# Canadian Daily Language Activities

—— Grade 1 ——

Written by Eleanor M. Summers

Our Canadian Daily Language Activities series provides short and quick opportunities for students to review and reinforce skills in punctuation, grammar, spelling, language and reading comprehension. The Bonus Activities that follow each week of skills are fun tasks such as word and vocabulary puzzles, figurative language and reading exercises. A short interesting fact about Canada is the finishing touch!

**ELEANOR M. SUMMERS** is a retired teacher who is still actively involved in education. She has created many resources in language, science and history. As a writer, she enjoys creating practical and thought-provoking resources for teachers and parents.

Copyright © On The Mark Press 2017

This publication may be reproduced under licence from Access Copyright, or with the express written permission of On The Mark Press, or as permitted by law. All rights are otherwise reserved, and no part of this publication may be reproduced, stored in a retrieval system, or transmitted in any form or by any means, electronic, mechanical, photocopying, scanning, recording or otherwise, except as specifically authorized.

All Rights Reserved.
Printed in Canada.

Published in Canada by:
On The Mark Press
Belleville, ON
www.onthemarkpress.com

Funded by the Government of Canada | Canadä

#OTM2160

**Topics cover:**
Needs and Characteristics of Living Things; and Exploring the Senses.

#OTM2152

**Topics cover:**
Daily and Seasonal Changes

154 pages include unit tests on: place value, counting, money, adding & subtracting to 10, linear measurement & area, capacity & mass quiz, time quiz, time, temperature & calendar, 2D geometry & symmetry, 3D geometry, location & movement, patterning, expressions & equality, data management and probability.

#K150

Just change the cover and stock # and keep the copy as it's the same for this book too.

#J181

Teacher Notes

# HOW TO USE CANADIAN DAILY LANGUAGE ACTIVITIES

This book is divided into 32 weekly sections.

Each weekly section provides daily skill review and assessment activities.

## ACTIVITIES 1 – 4:

Focus is on:
- punctuation, capitalization, grammar and spelling
- language and reading comprehension skills

## ACTIVITY 5:

Focus is on:
- a single language or reading skill

## BONUS ACTIVITY:

provides opportunities for extended activities
- word puzzles, vocabulary development
- spelling
- reading skills
- includes a short, interesting fact about Canada

## STUDENT PROGRESS CHART

Students may require a modelled example or individual assistance to complete their Progress Chart.

- Students record their daily score for each Language Activity.
- At the end of the week, they calculate their Total Score
- At the end of four weeks, students evaluate their performance.
- Students will require <u>one copy of page 3</u> and <u>three copies of page 4</u> to record results for entire 32 weeks. Teachers may wish to make back-to-back copies.

## TEACHER SUGGESTIONS

- All activities may be completed for each week or teachers may exclude some.
- New skills may be completed as a whole class activity.
- Bonus Activities may be used at teachers' discretion.
- Correcting student work together will help model the correct responses.
- Monitor student mastery of skills from information on the Student Progress Chart.

# _____ 'S PROGRESS CHART

How many did you get correct each day? Record your score on the chart.

| Week | Activity 1 | Activity 2 | Activity 3 | Activity 4 | Activity 5 | Total Score |
|---|---|---|---|---|---|---|
| # | /5 | /5 | /5 | /5 | /5 | /25 |

| Week | Activity 1 | Activity 2 | Activity 3 | Activity 4 | Activity 5 | Total Score |
|---|---|---|---|---|---|---|
| # | /5 | /5 | /5 | /5 | /5 | /25 |

| Week | Activity 1 | Activity 2 | Activity 3 | Activity 4 | Activity 5 | Total Score |
|---|---|---|---|---|---|---|
| # | /5 | /5 | /5 | /5 | /5 | /25 |

| Week | Activity 1 | Activity 2 | Activity 3 | Activity 4 | Activity 5 | Total Score |
|---|---|---|---|---|---|---|
| # | /5 | /5 | /5 | /5 | /5 | /25 |

My strongest skills are _____

My skills that need improvement are _____

The Bonus Activities I liked best are _____

| Week | Activity 1 | Activity 2 | Activity 3 | Activity 4 | Activity 5 | Total Score |
|---|---|---|---|---|---|---|
| # | /5 | /5 | /5 | /5 | /5 | /25 |

| Week | Activity 1 | Activity 2 | Activity 3 | Activity 4 | Activity 5 | Total Score |
|---|---|---|---|---|---|---|
| # | /5 | /5 | /5 | /5 | /5 | /25 |

| Week | Activity 1 | Activity 2 | Activity 3 | Activity 4 | Activity 5 | Total Score |
|---|---|---|---|---|---|---|
| # | /5 | /5 | /5 | /5 | /5 | /25 |

| Week | Activity 1 | Activity 2 | Activity 3 | Activity 4 | Activity 5 | Total Score |
|---|---|---|---|---|---|---|
| # | /5 | /5 | /5 | /5 | /5 | /25 |

My strongest skills are _____

My skills that need improvement are _____

The Bonus Activities I liked best are _____

# _____ 'S PROGRESS CHART

| Week | Activity 1 | Activity 2 | Activity 3 | Activity 4 | Activity 5 | Total Score |
|---|---|---|---|---|---|---|
| # | /5 | /5 | /5 | /5 | /5 | /25 |

| Week | Activity 1 | Activity 2 | Activity 3 | Activity 4 | Activity 5 | Total Score |
|---|---|---|---|---|---|---|
| # | /5 | /5 | /5 | /5 | /5 | /25 |

| Week | Activity 1 | Activity 2 | Activity 3 | Activity 4 | Activity 5 | Total Score |
|---|---|---|---|---|---|---|
| # | /5 | /5 | /5 | /5 | /5 | /25 |

| Week | Activity 1 | Activity 2 | Activity 3 | Activity 4 | Activity 5 | Total Score |
|---|---|---|---|---|---|---|
| # | /5 | /5 | /5 | /5 | /5 | /25 |

My strongest skills are _____

My skills that need improvement are _____

The Bonus Activities I liked best are _____

| Week | Activity 1 | Activity 2 | Activity 3 | Activity 4 | Activity 5 | Total Score |
|---|---|---|---|---|---|---|
| # | /5 | /5 | /5 | /5 | /5 | /25 |

| Week | Activity 1 | Activity 2 | Activity 3 | Activity 4 | Activity 5 | Total Score |
|---|---|---|---|---|---|---|
| # | /5 | /5 | /5 | /5 | /5 | /25 |

| Week | Activity 1 | Activity 2 | Activity 3 | Activity 4 | Activity 5 | Total Score |
|---|---|---|---|---|---|---|
| # | /5 | /5 | /5 | /5 | /5 | /25 |

| Week | Activity 1 | Activity 2 | Activity 3 | Activity 4 | Activity 5 | Total Score |
|---|---|---|---|---|---|---|
| # | /5 | /5 | /5 | /5 | /5 | /25 |

My strongest skills are _____

My skills that need improvement are _____

The Bonus Activities I liked best are _____

# DAILY LANGUAGE ACTIVITIES SKILLS LIST

This book provides many opportunities for practice of the following skills.

## Vocabulary and Word Skills

- vowel sounds/ consonant sounds
- spelling
- syllabication
- synonyms/antonyms/homonyms
- contractions
- rhyming words
- compound words
- word families

## Capitalization

- I
- beginning of sentences
- proper names/titles of people
- names of places
- titles of books, songs, poems
- names of days, months, holidays
- abbreviations

## Punctuation

- punctuation at the end of a sentence
- commas in a series
- commas in dates and addresses
- periods in abbreviations
- apostrophes in contractions
- apostrophes in possessives
- punctuation in a friendly letter

## Grammar and Word Usage

Parts of speech:

- nouns, pronouns
- singular/plural nouns
- possessive nouns
- adjectives: comparative, superlative
- verb forms
- adverbs
- double negatives
- subject – verb agreement
- identifying sentences: sentence vs not a sentence

## Reading Comprehension

- answering questions
- categorization
- predicting
- real or make-believe
- sequencing

## Reference Skills

- alphabetical order
- dictionary skills

Name: _____

**WEEK 6 — ACTIVITY 3**

**TOTAL /5**

Circle the word that means more than one.

1. cow    horse    pigs    hen

Circle the best word for each sentence.

2. The girls (is, are) playing in the yard.

3. She (is, are) going to help her mom.

Fix these sentences.

4. finn cant go withe us
   _____

5. is you leaving early in the morning
   _____

---

Name: _____

**WEEK 6 — ACTIVITY 4**

**TOTAL /5**

Fix these sentences.

1. do you has any new games
   _____

2. this here game is the bestest one
   _____

Sentence or not a sentence?

3. Stayed at home. _____

4. My mom is picking me up. _____

Circle the word that doesn't belong.

5. sun    moon    school    star

Name: _____

Write the words in correct order to make a sentence.

WEEK 6

ACTIVITY 5

TOTAL /5

1. tag   go   Let's   play   _____

2. lunch   I   my   ate   _____

3. Please   me   help   _____

4. fed   her   Dolly   cat   _____

5. popcorn   Susie   some   made   _____

---

Name: _____

**Bonus Activity:** Following Directions

Read the directions. Draw what you are asked to draw.

WEEK 6

BONUS ACTIVITY

1. Draw a tail on the dog.

2. Colour the dog light brown.

3. Draw a fancy collar on the dog.

4. Draw a dish with a bone in it.

5. Draw a smile on the dog's face.

**MY CANADA**
What did the man say when he finished building his igloo? That's an ice house!

Name: _____

**WEEK 7**
**ACTIVITY 1**
TOTAL /5

**Fix these sentences.**

1. cinderella weared glass slippers
   _____

2. her lost one wen her was running away
   _____

**Circle the correct word to fit each sentence.**

3. That ( was, were ) a funny joke.

4. Everyone ( is, are ) still laughing.

**Real or make-believe?**

5. A snowman might melt in the sun. _____

- - - - - - - - - - - - - - - - - - - - - - - - - - - - - - - - - - - - - - - - -

Name: _____

**WEEK 7**
**ACTIVITY 2**
TOTAL /5

**Write the opposite of each word.**

1. slow _____
2. sad _____

**Write two words in the 'ap' family.**

3. ap: _____

**Fix these sentences.**

4. will you cum withe me to the store
   _____

5. us can get sum ice cream
   _____

Name: _____

**WEEK 7**
**ACTIVITY 3**

**Circle the word that does not belong.**

1. birds    eggs    rock    nest

**Fix these sentences.**

2. lets gets pizza from pizza hut
   _____

3. well dad take us to pick it up
   _____

**Write the number of syllables (word parts) in each word.**

4. Woodstock _____

5. Wonderland _____

TOTAL /5

---

Name: _____

**WEEK 7**
**ACTIVITY 4**

**Fix these sentences.**

1. ms hunter read us the story, dandelion
   _____

2. it were about a lion trying to fix hims hair
   _____

**Circle the words that mean more than one.**

3. trees    leaf    branches    nests

**Circle the name that would come first in ABC order.**

4. Katie    Anna    Nancy

5. Kenny    Ryan    Josh

TOTAL /5

Name: _____

**Circle the best ending for each sentence.**

1. We plant seeds in the garden ... in the winter OR in the spring

2. Jill made a snow fort ... in the winter OR in the summer

3. We go swimming at the beach ... in the summer OR in the winter

4. Our grass starts to grow .... in the winter OR in the spring

5. Leaves fall from the trees ... in the winter OR in the fall

WEEK 7
ACTIVITY 5
TOTAL /5

---

Name: _____

**Bonus Activity:** Crack the Code

Use this code to find out what the sentence is saying.

WEEK 7

| 1 | 2 | 3 | 4 | 5 | 6 | 7 | 8 | 9 | 10 | 11 | 12 | 13 |
|---|---|---|---|---|---|---|---|---|----|----|----|----|
| a | b | c | d | e | f | g | h | i | j  | k  | l  | m  |
| 14 | 15 | 16 | 17 | 18 | 19 | 20 | 21 | 22 | 23 | 24 | 25 | 26 |
| n | o | p | q | r | s | t | u | v | w | x | y | z |

| 9 |  | 12 | 15 | 22 | 5 |  | 3 | 1 | 14 | 1 | 4 | 1 |  |
|---|--|----|----|----|----|--|---|---|----|---|---|---|--|
|   |  |    |    |    |    |  |   |   |    |   |   |   | ! |

Circle the name of Canada's capital. Toronto   Ottawa.

**MY CANADA**

Name: _____

**Fix these sentences.**

1. my grandpa live on a farm
   _____

2. him has cows, pigs and chickans
   _____

**Is it a sentence?**

3. My brother loves cookies.     Yes     No
4. Chocolate cookies.              Yes     No

**Write two words that rhyme with 'go'**

5. go : _____

WEEK 8
ACTIVITY 1
TOTAL /5

---

Name: _____

**Circle the correct word for each sentence.**

1. We walk ( to, two ) school each day.
2. I have ( to, two ) friends with me.

**Circle the word that is spelled correctly.**

3. stob     stap     stope     stop

**Fix these sentences.**

4. when well freddy get here
   _____

5. my kitten, mitten, have two black feet
   _____

WEEK 8
ACTIVITY 2
TOTAL /5

Name: _____

**WEEK 8**
**ACTIVITY 3**
**TOTAL /5**

**Circle the correct word for each sentence.**

1. Ms White is kind and (he, she) is a good teacher.
2. Mr. Earl sings and (he, she) plays the piano.

**Fix these sentences.**

3. little red riding hood walked in the woods
   _____

4. do you thinks her was afraid
   _____

**Write the two words for this contraction.**

5. can't _____

---

Name: _____

**WEEK 8**
**ACTIVITY 4**
**TOTAL /5**

**Fix these sentences.**

1. a berd is building a nest in our tree
   _____

2. does you think it will lay eggs there
   _____

**Write the word that best fits in the sentence.**

3. _____ the biggest puddle in our yard.
   Thats / Thats' / That's

**Circle what will happen next.**

4. Jake put on his jacket and then ...... he will go to bed  OR  he will go outside
5. The sky looked black and then ... it started to rain  OR  the bell rang

Name: _____

**Combine these sentences to make one good sentence.**

1. I like ice cream. I like chocolate the best.
   _____

2. Those puppies are cute. They are black lab pups.
   _____

3. My birthday is on Saturday. I am having a party.
   _____

4. We played a game of ball. We played in the backyard.
   _____

5. Aunt Jane is coming tomorrow. She is coming from Moncton.
   _____

WEEK 8
ACTIVITY 5
TOTAL /5

---

Name: _____

**Bonus Activity:** Find the People Words

Read the words in the boxes. If the word names a person, colour it orange.

WEEK 8

| mother | fireman | aunt | grandma |
| tree | rock | uncle | house |
| dog | father | grandpa | car |
| baker | kitten | horse | cowboy |

What is Canada's winter sport? *Hockey*.

**MY CANADA**

Name: _____

**WEEK 9 — ACTIVITY 1 — TOTAL /5**

Write a word that is opposite of each word.

1. hot _____
2. short _____

Fix these sentences.

3. i want to go to toronto
   _____

4. i want to sea a blue jays game
   _____

Circle the words that have the sound of 'c' in 'cat'

5. cent    cook    cold    circus

---

Name: _____

**WEEK 9 — ACTIVITY 2 — TOTAL /5**

Change the words to mean more than one.

1. boy _____
2. box _____

Real or make-believe?

3. It is cold at the North Pole. _____

Fix these sentences.

4. lets go to the lak
   _____

5. do you likes to swim at the beach
   _____

Name: _____

**WEEK 9**
**ACTIVITY 3**
**TOTAL /5**

**Circle Yes or No.**

1. Can a snowman dance?     Yes     No

**Fix these sentences.**

2. what colour are your new puppy

   _____

3. mines is brown and whit

   _____

**Make compound words.**

4. sun shine  _____

5. in side  _____

---

Name: _____

**WEEK 9**
**ACTIVITY 4**
**TOTAL /5**

**Fix these sentences.**

1. christmas day is in december

   _____

2. family day is in february

   _____

**What will happen next?**

3. Billy put milk in a glass.  Then ...... he will throw it out OR he will drink it

**Circle the best word.**

4. Our team (has, have) played a good game.

5. We (has, have) two new players.

Name: _____

Write the words where they belong.

apples   bread   coat   eggs   hat   meat
shirt   shoes

WEEK 9

ACTIVITY 5

TOTAL /5

| Things to Eat | Things to Wear |
| --- | --- |
| _____ | _____ |
| _____ | _____ |
| _____ | _____ |
| _____ | _____ |
| _____ | _____ |

---

Name: _____

**Bonus Activity:** At the Beach

WEEK 9

Look at the picture of the beach. Then draw pictures to show where you might see each object.

beach ball   sand pail   seashells   sand castle
umbrella

What day is Canada's birthday?   April 4   July 1

**MY CANADA**

Name: _____

**WEEK 10**
**ACTIVITY 1**
**TOTAL /5**

Write two words for each of these word families.

1. - ad _____
2. - et _____

Fix these sentences.

3. today are a sunny dai
   _____

4. does you wants to play at the park
   _____

Circle the correct spelling.

5. git    gat    get    gete

---

Name: _____

**WEEK 10**
**ACTIVITY 2**
**TOTAL /5**

Circle the best word for each sentence.

1. (I, Me) need a new pair of boots.
2. Mom will buy (I, me) some on Saturday.

Circle the word that doesn't belong.

3. red    orange    apple    yellow

Fix these sentences.

4. my grandma live in england
   _____

5. i is going to see her in july
   _____

Name: _____

**WEEK 10**
**ACTIVITY 3**
**TOTAL /5**

Circle the word that comes first in alphabetical order.

1. make    dog    food    head

**Fix these sentences.**

2. cats likes to chase mouses

_____

3. my cat, flash, hunts in our yerd

_____

**Circle Yes or No.**

4. Summer is in July.    Yes    No
5. Winter is in August.    Yes    No

---

Name: _____

**WEEK 10**
**ACTIVITY 4**
**TOTAL /5**

**Fix these sentences.**

1. is you going to sea the movie

_____

2. we is going on friday night

_____

**Circle the words that rhyme with 'can'**

3. man    and    fan    sat    pan

**Is the sentence a question?  Circle Yes or No.**

4. How long is the story    Yes    No
5. I want to go home    Yes    No

SSR1144   ISBN: 9781771587303 © On The Mark Press          35

Name: _____

**Make these sentences into one good sentence.**

1. A cat has fur. A dog has fur.
   _____

2. I like baseball. I like soccer.
   _____

3. I have a sister. I have a brother.
   _____

4. Dan is my friend. Ann is my friend.
   _____

5. Sue likes apples. Sue likes grapes.
   _____

WEEK 10
ACTIVITY 5
TOTAL /5

---

Name: _____

**Bonus Activity:** Outdoor Fun

**Find and circle these words in the Word Search puzzle.**

fish   bike   run   hike   swim   camp   sail

| a | h | k | w | r | u | n | a |
|---|---|---|---|---|---|---|---|
| f | i | s | h | e | f | c | w |
| f | k | n | l | p | l | a | y |
| h | e | l | s | w | i | m | r |
| y | q | e | a | p | h | p | u |
| t | r | b | i | k | e | w | i |
| e | i | p | l | a | i | p | h |

WEEK 10

Basketball was invented by a Canadian, James Naismith.

**MY CANADA**

Name: _____

**Fix these sentences.**

1. i dont wawnt to play socker
   _____

2. can patti and ali cum over tonite
   _____

**Circle the words that rhyme with ' book'**

3. cook    took    soon    look

4. shook    loop    crook    boot

**Write the word that is missing.**

5. Dan _____ coming to my house to play.
   are / were / is

WEEK 11
ACTIVITY 1
TOTAL /5

---

Name: _____

**Circle sentence or not a sentence.**

1. Rained all day          Sentence    Not a sentence
2. We saw a rainbow in the sky    Sentence    Not a sentence

**Fix these sentences.**

3. the grinch is a christmas story
   _____

4. grandma smith is comin on sunday
   _____

**Circle real or make-believe.**

5. Beavers lay eggs.          Real        Make-believe

WEEK 11
ACTIVITY 2
TOTAL /5

Name: _____

**Fix these sentences.**

1. do you hide eggs for easter
   _____

2. i like huntin for thum
   _____

**Circle the best word.**

3. (To, Two) boys ran down the street.

4. They live next door (too, to) me.

**Circle the correct word on the line.**

5. That puppy is the _____ one.
   small / smaller / smallest

WEEK 11
ACTIVITY 3
TOTAL /5

---

Name: _____

**Circle Real or Make-believe.**

1. Canada geese fly south.          Real     Make-believe
2. Canada geese lay golden eggs.    Real     Make-believe

**Fix these sentences.**

3. i have a little brother named bobby
   _____

4. him is too years old
   _____

**Circle the correct word.**

5. We (paints, painted) the fence.

WEEK 11
ACTIVITY 4
TOTAL /5

Name: _____

## Growing a Pumpkin

**Number the sentences in the correct order.**

_____ Plant a pumpkin seed in the ground.

_____ Dig a small hole in the ground.

_____ Water the ground where the seed is.

_____ Cover the seed with dirt.

_____ Wait for the pumpkin plant to grow.

WEEK 11
ACTIVITY 5
TOTAL /5

---

Name: _____

**Bonus Activity:** Action Words

Write a word from the Word Box to match the picture.

Word Box:   dig   smile   read   run   sing.

WEEK 11
BONUS ACTIVITY

The Rocky Mountains stretch 4800 km.   **MY CANADA**

Name: _____

**Circle Sentence or Not a sentence.**

1. There are robin eggs in the nest.    Sentence    Not a sentence

**Fix these sentences.**

2. monday morning jen will go to school
_____

3. her are in grade one
_____

**Circle the words that rhyme with the first word.**

4. feet:    let    beet    meet    net    greet
5. blow:    grow    now    snow    flow

WEEK 12
ACTIVITY 1
TOTAL /5

---

Name: _____

**Fix these sentences.**

1. i can rid a bike
_____

2. i hop i gets a new one soon
_____

**Circle the word that is spelled correctly in each row.**

3. thay    thye    they    theey
4. wint    whent    wehnt    went

**Circle the best word.**

5. The elephant is the (big, bigger, biggest) animal in the zoo.

WEEK 12
ACTIVITY 2
TOTAL /5

Name: _____

**WEEK 12**

**ACTIVITY 3**

**Fix these sentences.**

1. my dog cleo had for puppies
   _____

2. i went to keep the blak one
   _____

**TOTAL /5**

**Circle the best answer.**

3. Fluffy is playing with a toy mouse. Is Fluffy ..... a cat?   OR   a bird?

4. We are wet.  We are at the beach. Are we .... talking?   OR   swimming?

**Circle the words that need capital letters.**

5. i am going to toronto on monday.

---

Name: _____

**WEEK 12**

**ACTIVITY 4**

**Fix these sentences.**

1. remembrance day is november 11
   _____

2. we think about our canadian soldiers
   _____

**TOTAL /5**

**How many word parts do you hear?**

3. Montreal _____

4. Ottawa _____

**Number these words in alphabetical order.**

5. ..... carrot     ..... apple     ..... banana     .... date

Name: _____

**Circle the part that tells <u>how</u>.**

1. The girls began to sing loudly.

2. The man was in a hurry.

3. The mouse ran away quickly.

4. Hank told his story sadly.

5. Annie smiled happily when she won.

WEEK 12

ACTIVITY 5

TOTAL /5

---

Name: _____

**Bonus Activity:** Compound Words

Compound words are made up of two small words. Read the words in the boxes.

If the word is a compound word, colour the box orange.

| outside | movie | sunshine |
|---------|-------|----------|
| puppy | inside | fort |
| today | castle | football |

WEEK 12

What TV show does a Canada Goose watch? *The feather report!*

**MY CANADA**

Name: _____

**Circle the word that means the same as 'fast'**

1. pink    little    quick    tall

**Fix these sentences.**

2. does him like chocolate cake
   _____

3. january is a very cold month
   _____

**Read the sentences. Circle Yes or No.**

4. If it rains, the ground is wet.     Yes    No
5. A car can drive to the moon.     Yes    No

WEEK 13
ACTIVITY 1
TOTAL /5

---

Name: _____

**Write the two words that make each contraction.**

1. won't _____
2. they'll _____

**Fix these sentences.**

3. do mary like to shop in regina
   _____

4. yes, her goes with her sister, lizzie
   _____

**Write the missing word on the line.**    tall    taller    tallest

5. My brother is _____ than me.

WEEK 13
ACTIVITY 2
TOTAL /5

Name: _____

**Circle the correct meaning for the underlined word.**

1. Sally has long brown <u>hair</u>.

    (a) a rabbit    (b) what grows on your head

**Correct these sentences.**

2. has you read the story <u>hop on pop</u>

   _____

3. i likes the book, <u>red fish, blue fish</u>

   _____

**Circle the words that rhyme.**

4. bump    dump    sum    lump

5. ten    red    bed    can

**WEEK 13**

**ACTIVITY 3**

**TOTAL /5**

---

Name: _____

**Circle the word that is spelled correctly.**

1. bal    boll    bole    ball

**Fix these sentences.**

2. what do you eats on thanksgiving

   _____

3. christmas am in december

   _____

**Circle Real or Make-believe.**

4. The little kittens lost their mittens.    Real    Make-believe

5. The bird flew high in the sky.    Real    Make-believe

**WEEK 13**

**ACTIVITY 4**

**TOTAL /5**

Name: _____

**WEEK 13**
**ACTIVITY 5**
**TOTAL /5**

Write the words in the correct group.

strawberries   grass   cherries   stop sign   lime   plant

**Green Things**                      **Red Things**

_____          _____
_____          _____
_____          _____
_____          _____
_____          _____
_____          _____
_____          _____

---

Name: _____

**WEEK 13**
**BONUS ACTIVITY**

**Bonus Activity:** Vowel Maze

The vowels are: a  e  i  o  u

Colour the boxes that have vowels to make a path.

START

| a | n | u | e | o | w | q |
| e | o | i | p | a | u | i |
| d | m | z | h | t | k | a |

FINISH

*The first Calgary Stampede was held over 100 years ago.*

**MY CANADA**

Name: _____

**WEEK 14**

**Fix these sentences.**

1. monday are the first school day of the week
   _____

2. on sunday we is going to see grandma
   _____

**ACTIVITY 1**

**TOTAL /5**

**How many word parts do you hear?**

3. buffalo _____

**Write the word that means more than one.**

4. one baby        two _____

5. one fox         two _____

---

Name: _____

**WEEK 14**

**Fix these sentences.**

1. the bestest day of the week is saturday
   _____

2. what do you like to do on saturday
   _____

**ACTIVITY 2**

**TOTAL /5**

**Circle the best word.**

3. My mom is busy. (Her, She) is making lunch.

4. Our family is big. (It, That) has seven people.

**Circle True or False.**

5. Beavers are good swimmers.        True        False

Name: _____

**WEEK 14 ACTIVITY 3**

**Circle Real or Make-believe.**

1. The tiny mouse ran under the bed.   Real   Make-believe
2. 'You can't catch me!' the mouse called.   Real   Make-believe

**Fix these sentences.**

3. we clapped at the ende of the shoe
   _____

4. it were about a lost princess named esmai
   _____

**Tell if these words are the same or opposite.**

5. cold, hot _____

TOTAL /5

---

Name: _____

**WEEK 14 ACTIVITY 4**

**Fix these sentences.**

1. i love to swum at the beach
   _____

2. we is going there on friday
   _____

**Write the pronoun for the underlined words.**

3. The <u>dog</u> is barking. _____

4. <u>My dad</u> will tell it to stop. _____

**Tell the meaning of the underlined word.**

5. What a big <u>herd</u> of cattle! _____

TOTAL /5

Name: _____

## What Goes ........ ?

Draw a line from the 'sound' words to the correct picture.

1. Drip, drip
2. Toot, toot
3. Buzz, buzz
4. Boom, boom
5. Ring, ring

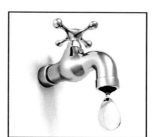

WEEK 14
ACTIVITY 5
TOTAL /5

---

Name: _____

## Bonus Activity: 'ch' Word Scramble

Unscramble these words to make words to match the pictures. Write your answer in the box.

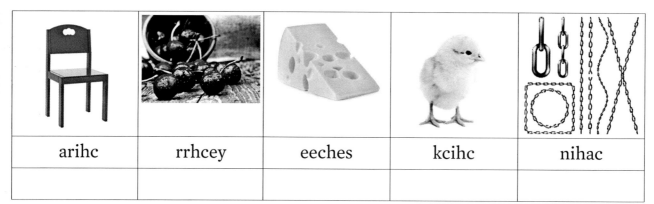

| arihc | rrhcey | eeches | kcihc | nihac |
|-------|--------|--------|-------|-------|
|       |        |        |       |       |

**MY CANADA**

Dog **sledding** is a popular sport in Canada's North.

Name: _____

**WEEK 15 — ACTIVITY 1 — TOTAL /5**

Circle the words that rhyme with the first word.

1. cab:   dab   tap   crab   dad   slab
2. ring:  sing  bring  sang  sap  zing

Circle the correct abbreviation for Monday

3. Mo.   Mond.   Mon.   Mony.

Fix these sentences.

4. i made a jack-o-lantern for hallowe'en
_____

5. did it has a scary face
_____

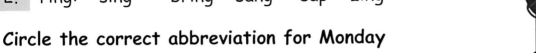

---

Name: _____

**WEEK 15 — ACTIVITY 2 — TOTAL /5**

Circle Sentence or Not a sentence.

1. The truck zoomed down the road.    Sentence    Not a sentence

Fix these sentences.

2. today we is going to the dentist
_____

3. my sister, lily, doesnt want to go
_____

Circle the word that is spelled correctly.

4. purpel   perple   purple   perpule
5. grean   grene   grein   green

Name: _____

**WEEK 15**
**ACTIVITY 3**
**TOTAL /5**

**Circle Yes or No.**

1. Is an ant small?      Yes      No

**Circle the best word for each sentence.**

2. Mr. Brown is my teacher. (He, Him) reads us good stories.

3. Mom made our lunch. (Her, She) is a good cook.

**Fix these sentences.**

4. what day is tonys party
_____

5. me thinks it is on friday
_____

---

Name: _____

**WEEK 15**
**ACTIVITY 4**
**TOTAL /5**

**Circle the part that would happen first.**

1. Mom lit the candles.      We sang 'Happy Birthday'.
2. The runners took off.      The starter yelled 'GO!'

**Fix these sentences.**

3. well you come to the library withe me
_____

4. i is looking for a book called <u>knock, knock jokes</u>
_____

**How many syllables (word parts) do you hear?**

5. Halifax _____

Name: _____

**WEEK 15**
**ACTIVITY 5**
**TOTAL /5**

Write the words in their correct group.

bike    flower    shovel    father    cat    ball

| Living Things | Non-living Things |
|---|---|
| _____ | _____ |
| _____ | _____ |
| _____ | _____ |
| _____ | _____ |
| _____ | _____ |

---

Name: _____

**WEEK 15**
**BONUS ACTIVITY**

**Bonus Activity:** I See Red!

**Look for words that name foods that are <u>red</u>.**

apple   cherry   jam   jello   lollipop   plum   spaghetti   tomato

| a | c | h | e | c | z | f | l | a |
|---|---|---|---|---|---|---|---|---|
| s | p | a | g | h | e | t | t | i |
| t | l | p | d | e | x | o | a | k |
| g | u | p | k | r | v | m | a | j |
| h | m | l | i | r | n | a | h | e |
| b | k | e | q | y | b | t | e | l |
| l | o | l | l | i | p | o | p | l |
| u | e | a | m | r | q | j | k | o |

How do bees get around Canada in the winter? On Bee-doos!    **MY CANADA**

Name: _____

**Where would it happen?**

1. We sat quietly as Ms Gray began to speak.   Classroom   Playground

**Circle the best word to fit in these sentences.**

2. Sally got a new coat. (She, Her) picked a red one.

3. Tommy's new puppy is all black. (That, It) is very cute.

**Fix these sentences.**

4. my new bake are red and black

_____

5. i gots it fer my birthday on saturday

_____

WEEK 16
ACTIVITY 1
TOTAL /5

---

Name: _____

**Real or make-believe?**

1. The elephant danced along the street.    Real    Make-believe

**Circle the words that rhyme with the first word.**

2. find:   kind    tend    sand    mind

3. that:   bat    mat    set    bit

**Fix these sentences.**

4. i plays baseball on monday and thursday

_____

5. would you likes to join our teem

_____

WEEK 16
ACTIVITY 2
TOTAL /5

Name: _____

**Write a word that is the opposite of:**

1. night _____

2. hot _____

**Circle the letters that are capitals.**

3.   A   q   L   R   d   f   C   b   T

**Fix these sentences.**

4.   pennys new mittens is missing

_____

5.   lets help she looks for them

_____

WEEK 16
ACTIVITY 3
TOTAL /5

---

Name: _____

**Fix these sentences.**

1.   dad leaved for werk early today

_____

2.   brush yer tooths before you go to bed

_____

**Circle the sentence to tell what happens next.**

3.   Mom called my name. So ...... I answered her.   OR   I went outside.

4.   Dan lost his pencil. So ...... He jumped up and down.   OR   He looked for it.

**Write the word that means just one.**

5.   toys _____

WEEK 16
ACTIVITY 4
TOTAL /5

Name: _____

**These students are in my class. Write their names in ABC order.**

Donnie   Cara   Amy   Gary   Logan   Fanny

WEEK 16

ACTIVITY 5

TOTAL /5

1. _____
2. _____
3. _____
4. _____
5. _____
6. _____

---

Name: _____

WEEK 16

**Bonus Activity:** Looking for Shapes

1. Colour the squares yellow.
2. Colour the circles green.
3. Colour the triangle blue.
4. Colour the rectangle red.

Nunavut means 'our land'.   **MY CANADA**

**WEEK 17 — ACTIVITY 1** — TOTAL /5

Name: _____

**Fix these sentences.**

1. dad losted hims keys on sunday
   _____

2. where is you going today
   _____

**Circle the words that need capital letters.**

3. home    canada    farm    toronto
4. kitten    susie    alice    horse

**Write two words in the -ent family.**

5. _____

---

**WEEK 17 — ACTIVITY 2** — TOTAL /5

Name: _____

**Circle the words that name animals.**

1. fox    den    kittens    hole    beaver

**Fix these sentences.**

2. did you gets a letter in the mail
   _____

3. grandma sands us a card on our birthday
   _____

**Where does the apostrophe go?**

4. Jills dolls
5. Timmys toys

Name: _____

**WEEK 17 · ACTIVITY 3 · TOTAL /5**

**Circle the best words.**

1. (Me and you, You and I) can go to the movies.
2. (He and she, Him and Her) play baseball on my team.

**Circle the word that is spelled correctly.**

3. thees     thiz     this     thith

**Fix these sentences.**

4. will you please hand me the book
   _____

5. ill brung it to you now
   _____

---

Name: _____

**WEEK 17 · ACTIVITY 4 · TOTAL /5**

**Real or make-believe?**

1. The cow jumped over the moon.     Real     Make-believe
2. The farmer milks his cows.            Real     Make-believe

**Fix these sentences.**

3. grandma gots a new sun hat
   _____

4. it are red blue and yellow
   _____

**Write a word that means the same as**

5. little _____

**Cause and Effect**

Draw a line to match each cause with its effect.

1. If you step in the puddle          * it will whine
2. If you run fast                    * your shoes will get wet.
3. If you don't feed your puppy       * she will be happy.
4. If you play our game               * you will win the race.
5. If you help your Mom               * you will have fun.

WEEK 17
ACTIVITY 5
TOTAL /5

---

**Bonus Activity:** Colour Code

Use this code to spell the names of these colours. Colour each circle the correct colour.

| 1 | 2 | 3 | 4 | 5 | 6 | 7 | 8 | 9 | 10 | 11 | 12 | 13 | 14 | 15 | 16 | 17 | 18 | 19 | 20 | 21 | 22 | 23 | 24 | 25 | 26 |
|---|---|---|---|---|---|---|---|---|----|----|----|----|----|----|----|----|----|----|----|----|----|----|----|----|----|
| a | b | c | d | e | f | g | h | i | j  | k  | l  | m  | n  | o  | p  | q  | r  | s  | t  | u  | v  | w  | x  | y  | z  |

1. __ __ __ __ __ ○
   2   12   21   5

2. __ __ __ ○
   18  5   4

3. __ __ __ __ __ __ ○
   25  5  12  12  15  23

WEEK 17

*Many dinosaur bones have been found in Alberta.*

**MY CANADA**

Name: _____

**WEEK 18**
**ACTIVITY 1**
**TOTAL /5**

Write the correct word on the line.

1. Alex _____ sick yesterday.    was    were
2. He _____ better today.    feel    feels

Fix these sentences.

3. did theo gets a new toy
   _____

4. him want a red firetruck
   _____

Circle the compound words..

5. We play baseball and basketball.

---

Name: _____

**WEEK 18**
**ACTIVITY 2**
**TOTAL /5**

Circle the words that need capital letters..

1. the twins are tim and tom.
2. they live on oak street.
   _____

Fix these sentences.

3. sandys favourite colour is blew
   _____

4. what well you do this weekend
   _____

Sentence or Not a sentence?

5. The last day of school    Sentence    Not a sentence

Name: _____

**WEEK 18 — ACTIVITY 3**

**Fix these sentences.**

1. mike and hims dad is going to toronto
   _____

2. they is going to a blue jays ball game
   _____

**How many syllables (word parts) in each word?**

3. Saturday _____

4. sunshine _____

**Circle the words that rhyme.**

5. day    date    play    dad    say

TOTAL /5

---

Name: _____

**WEEK 18 — ACTIVITY 4**

**Number these words in alphabetical order.**

1. ...... soon    ......den    ...... hunt    ....... bug

**Fix these sentences.**

2. i seen a robin yesterday
   _____

3. it were building a nest in our bigg tree
   _____

**Write two words for each contraction.**

4. isn't _____ and _____

5. don't _____ and _____

TOTAL /5

Name: _____

**WEEK 18**

**ACTIVITY 5**

**TOTAL /5**

Number the sentences in the order they would happen.

_____ The bird found some string.

_____ The bird looked for a good place for a nest.

_____ The bird flew up into our big tree.

_____ The bird flew down.

_____ The bird is building a nest

---

Name: _____

**WEEK 18**

**BONUS ACTIVITY**

**Bonus Activity:** Read, Draw and Colour

Read each sentence. Draw and colour a picture in the box.

| | | |
|---|---|---|
| | | |
| It rained all day. | The wind blew hard. | A branch broke on our tree. |

*What is a Canadian cat's favourite sport? Mice hockey!*

**MY CANADA**

Name: _____

**WEEK 19**

**Fix these sentences.**

1. this are a good book
   _____

2. it are called <u>danny and the dinosaurs</u>
   _____

**What is this person doing?**

3. Jump in and make a big splash!
   _____

**Write the best word on the line.**

4. We went to _____ house.
   there / their

5. Go stand over _____
   there / their

**ACTIVITY 1**

**TOTAL /5**

---

Name: _____

**WEEK 19**

**Circle the word that is spelled correctly.**

1. tyme    tiem    time    teim

**Fix these sentences.**

2. tami singed a good song
   _____

3. we all claped and claped for her
   _____

**Circle the words that go together.**

4. apple    grapes    grass    banana    sky
5. kittens    shoes    cars    puppies    lambs

**ACTIVITY 2**

**TOTAL /5**

SSR1144   ISBN: 9781771587303 © On The Mark Press

Name: _____

**Circle the words that tell about a duck.**

1. quacks   sings   swims   flies   talks

**Write the best word on the line.**

2. We _____ the cookies.
   take / took

3. Will you _____ this dish, please?
   take / took

**Fix these sentences.**

4. come with my to sea the chicks
   _____

5. isnt they fluffy little birds
   _____

WEEK 19
ACTIVITY 3
TOTAL /5

---

Name: _____

**Who might be saying the following?**

1. 'Brush your teeth before you go to bed' _____
2. 'Listen carefully, class' _____

**Circle the word that is spelled correctly.**

3. doos   duz   does   duse

**Fix these sentences.**

4. our teem is called the red runners
   _____

5. we wears red hates and red shirts
   _____

WEEK 19
ACTIVITY 4
TOTAL /5

Name: _____

**WEEK 19**

Read this address. Circle the words that need capitals. Write the capital letter above the small letter.

miss     sophie     greene

5     pine     street

kingston,     ontario.

ACTIVITY 5

TOTAL /5

---

Name: _____

**WEEK 19**

**Bonus Activity:** Tell Me the Time

1. Write the numbers on the clock.

2. Draw on the hands in red to show what time you go to bed.

3. Draw on hands in blue to show what time you get up.

4. Circle the even numbers.

The *zipper* was invented by a Canadian.

**MY CANADA**

Name: _____

**WEEK 20**

**ACTIVITY 1**

**What do the underlined words mean?**

1. Jack runs <u>like a deer.</u> _____

**Write the two words that make each compound word..**

2. playground _____ and _____

3. beehive _____ and _____

**POUTINE**

**Fix these sentences.**

4. me and me friends went to see <u>frozen</u>
   _____

5. we liked elsa and olaf the bestest
   _____

**TOTAL /5**

---

Name: _____

**WEEK 20**

**ACTIVITY 2**

**POUTINE**

**Fix these sentences.**

1. lets go skateing on sunday
   _____

2. well you plese call dana for me
   _____

**How many syllables (word parts) in each word?**

3. bobsled _____

4. tennis _____

**Circle the abbreviation for 'Street'**

5. Str.    Stre.    St.    Stret.

**TOTAL /5**

64    SSR1144   ISBN: 9781771587303   © On The Mark Press

Name: _____

**POUTINE**

WEEK **20**

ACTIVITY **3**

TOTAL **/5**

Write the opposite for:

1. go _____

**Fix these sentences.**

2. i likes to play with me friend, jeff

   _____

3. hims are a nice boy and are funny

   _____

**What will happen next?**

4. I filled my glass with milk. Then ...... I poured it out.   OR   I drank it.

5. The toast popped up. Then ...... I buttered it.   OR   I put it in a glass.

---

Name: _____

**POUTINE**

WEEK **20**

ACTIVITY **4**

TOTAL **/5**

**Circle the name that comes first in ABC order.**

1. Randy     Kayla     Sam
2. Brock     Abe     Carl

**Fix these sentences.**

3. mr and mrs lee live next door

   _____

4. how long has thay lived their

   _____

**Circle the words that do not belong.**

5. shoes     socks     carrots     hat     dog     coat

Name: _____

**WEEK 20**

**ACTIVITY 5**

**TOTAL /5**

Compound words are two words joined together to make a new word. Write the correct compound word in these sentences.

flashlight    sunflower    cowboy    pancake    raincoat

1. Wear your _____ and you won't get wet.

2. We give _____ seeds to the birds.

3. Take a _____ so you can see in the dark.

4. I had a big _____ for breakfast.

5. My uncle is a _____ on a ranch.

POUTINE

---

Name: _____

**WEEK 20**

**BONUS ACTIVITY**

**Bonus Activity:** Your Story

Look at each picture. Write a good sentence about each picture in the box below it.

_____

_____

_____

POUTINE

Poutine was first made in Canada.

**MY CANADA**

66    SSR1144   ISBN: 9781771587303 © On The Mark Press

Name: _____

**Circle Sentence or Not a sentence.**

1. Hot dogs for lunch    Sentence    Not a Sentence
2. I love chocolate milk!    Sentence    Not a sentence

**Fix these sentences.**

3. lets watches a movie on tv
   _____

4. does you want sum popcorn
   _____

**Circle the words that need capital letters.**

5. mr    dr    town    car    mrs

WEEK **21**

ACTIVITY **1**

TOTAL **/5**

---

Name: _____

**Fix these sentences.**

1. judy drawed a goode picture
   _____

2. it were a rainbow in the skye
   _____

**Give two words that rhyme with each of these words.**

3. dip _____

4. out _____

**Tell where this event is happening.**

5. We are buying apples, bread and milk. _____

WEEK **21**

ACTIVITY **2**

TOTAL **/5**

Name: _____

**WEEK 21**

**Circle the words that tell about a puppy.**

1. plays    talks    jumps    laugh    licks

_____

**Fix these sentences.**

2. i gots a letter frum sarah

_____

3. her live in calgary, alberta

_____

**Real or make-believe?**

4. I made a snowman in the summer.    Real    Make-believe
5. Apples are good for you to eat.    Real    Make-believe

ACTIVITY 3

TOTAL /5

---

Name: _____

**WEEK 21**

**Fix these sentences.**

1. uncle fred are the bestest uncle

_____

2. him takes me go-cart raceing

_____

**Circle the best word.**

3. We (was, were) all going out to play.
4. Marty (was, were) 'It' for tag.

**Circle the word that means more than one box.**

5. boxs    boxess    boxes    box

ACTIVITY 4

TOTAL /5

Name: _____

## Canada Quiz

Read each sentence. Circle Yes or No.

**WEEK 21**

**ACTIVITY 5**

**TOTAL /5**

1. Canada's flag is red and green.    Yes    No

2. Canada has three seasons.    Yes    No

3. Polar bears live in Canada.    Yes    No

4. Beavers live in Canada.    Yes    No

5. Mounties are police officers.    Yes    No

---

Name: _____

**Bonus Activity:**  'Bl' Blends

Read the clues.  Use these blends in the puzzle.

**WEEK 21**

| Clue | black | blow | blind | blaze | blue |
|---|---|---|---|---|---|
| 1. I am the colour of the sky. | | | | | |
| 2. The wind does this. | | | | | |
| 3. I am flames or a fire. | | | | | |
| 4. The opposite of 'white'. | | | | | |
| 5. Not able to see. | | | | | |

**MY CANADA**

*What do you call a very cold teddy bear? A Teddy Brrrr!*

Name: _____

**WEEK 22**

**ACTIVITY 1**

**TOTAL /5**

Circle the words that mean more than one.

1. teeth     tooth
2. man     men

Circle the word that comes first in ABC order.

3. mist     flip     bush     shell

Fix these sentences.

4. the girls has read the poem 'anna banana'
   _____

5. them says it when thay is skipping
   _____

---

Name: _____

**WEEK 22**

**ACTIVITY 2**

**TOTAL /5**

How many syllables (word parts) are in this word?

1. terrible _____

Circle the words that are spelled correctly.

2. frum     frm     from     fram
3. abuot     about     abot     abut

Fix these sentences.

4. jon can do it more better
   _____

5. we wants to go to the parke on sunday
   _____

Name: _____

**What will happen next?**

1. Mom gave me a loonie for helping. So ...... I will put it in my bank. **OR** I will throw it away.

2. I put on my boots and raincoat. So ..... It must be sunny outside. **OR** It must be raining.

**Circle the words that go together.**

3.  blue    truck    yellow    bike    orange

**Fix these sentences.**

4. i goes to hill park school

_____

5. it are on maple street on windsor, ontario

_____

WEEK 22
ACTIVITY 3
TOTAL /5

---

Name: _____

**Tell what this person's job would be.**

1. He blows a whistle to stop the game. _____

**Fix these sentences.**

2. well patty come to bettys party

_____

3. her plans to cum if her mom let her

_____

**Circle the best word.**

4. Sam doesn't have (no, any) money.

5. (Any, No) treats for him today!

WEEK 22
ACTIVITY 4
TOTAL /5

Name: _____

The vowels are: a e i o u. Fill in the vowels for these words.

1. m _____ th _____ r

2. f _____ th _____ r

3. s _____ st _____ r

4. _____ ncl _____

5. _____ _____ nt

**WEEK 22**

ACTIVITY 5

TOTAL /5

---

Name: _____

**Bonus Activity:** Things I Like to Do

Read the words. Draw your Ideas.

**WEEK 22**

| | | |
|---|---|---|
| | | |
| Something I like to do by myself. | Something I like to do with my family. | Something I like to do with my friends. |

**MY CANADA**

Baby beavers are called kittens.

Name: _____

**WEEK 23**
**ACTIVITY 1**
**TOTAL /5**

**Fix these sentences.**

1. cud you help the new boy withe hims buks
   _____

2. him neds a friend to play withe too
   _____

**Real or Make-believe?**

3. The sky is falling!
   _____

**Write the correct word on the line.**

4. Bobby has _____ toys with him.
                       **her / his**

5. Annie plays with _____ dolls.
                       **her / his**

---

Name: _____

**WEEK 23**
**ACTIVITY 2**
**TOTAL /5**

**Fix these sentences.**

1. well you looke fore the ball i lost
   _____

2. it are red and blew with yellow stars
   _____

**Circle the words that are names of people.**

3. My sister and brother are watching a movie.

4. Chris and Hank like to play ball.

**Write the contraction made from these two words.**

5. let us _____

Name: _____

**Correct these sentences.**

1. chad and me cant go to the show
   _____

2. has you seed the movie, boss baby
   _____

**Circle the words that are opposites**

3. black    red    purple    white

**Real or make-believe?**

4. The boy climbed to the top of the tree.    Real    Make-believe

5. Jack climbed to the top of the beanstalk.    Real __ Make-believe

WEEK 23
ACTIVITY 3
TOTAL /5

---

Name: _____

**Circle the correct spelling.**

1. sckool    sckul    school    skool

**Write the word meaning more than one.**

2. one party _____

3. one leaf _____

**Fix these sentences.**

4. jane winned the mostest ribbons for running
   _____

5. is her the fasteste gerl in your classe
   _____

WEEK 23
ACTIVITY 4
TOTAL /5

Name: _____

**Number the sentences in the order they happen.**

_____ It began to rain and rain.

_____ The rain stopped.

_____ The sky was full of dark clouds.

_____ I saw a rainbow in the sky.

_____ I looked out the window.

WEEK **23**

ACTIVITY **5**

TOTAL **/5**

---

Name: _____

**Bonus Activity:** Homonym Word Search

Homonyms are words that sound the same. Find and circle these homonyms in the puzzle.

| blue | week | meat | be | bear | to, too, two |
| blew | weak | meet | bee | bare | |

| b | e | e | m | w | e | e | k |
|---|---|---|---|---|---|---|---|
| l | t | r | m | b | d | s | t |
| u | w | b | e | a | r | z | o |
| e | o | b | a | r | e | n | o |
| f | h | k | t | e | m | z | w |
| m | t | o | n | b | i | e | w |
| w | e | a | k | v | w | x | b |
| p | e | r | t | y | z | a | c |
| q | m | s | u | w | o | n | d |

WEEK **23**

The maple *leaf* on Canada's flag has 11 points.   **MY CANADA**

Name: _____

**WEEK 24 — ACTIVITY 1 — TOTAL /5**

Why did dad stop? Underline the words that tell why.

1. Dad stopped because the light turned red.

Fix these sentences.

2. abi runned the fastest of all the gerls
   _____

3. did her wine every race
   _____

Circle Sentence or Not a sentence.

4. Out in the backyard.   Sentence   Not a sentence
5. We like to play tag.   Sentence   Not a sentence

---

Name: _____

**WEEK 24 — ACTIVITY 2 — TOTAL /5**

Circle the word that means more than one.

1. foots     feets     feet
2. wifes     wives     wiffes

Fix these sentences.

3. pete is my bestest frend
   _____

4. tell use all abowt yur gaim
   _____

Circle the rhyming words.

5. bee     tell     see     gone     wee

Name: _____

**Real or make-believe?**

1. Tommy climbed the big tree.   Real   Make-believe

**Fix these sentences.**

2. i rided me bike to larrys house

_____

3. does him live vary far away

_____

**What will happen next?  Circle the correct sentence.**

4. Mom took out her cookie cookbook. So ... She is going shopping. OR She is going to bake cookies.

5. Sally writes a note on a card to her Grandma. So ..... She will mail it. OR She will lose it.

WEEK 24
ACTIVITY 3
TOTAL /5

---

Name: _____

**Fix these sentences.**

1. we hav went to all the soccer gaims

_____

2. we cheer eech time our teem scores

_____

**Circle the correct abbreviation for each word.**

3. Monday :   Mond.   MON   Mon.

4. October :   OCT   Octo.   Oct.

**Underline the words that name animals.**

5. There are pigs, cows and horses on Grandpa's farm.

WEEK 24
ACTIVITY 4
TOTAL /5

Name: _____

Write the words in their correct group.

| | Sweet Things | Sour Things |
|---|---|---|
| sugar | | |
| lemons | _____ | _____ |
| grapefruit | _____ | _____ |
| candy | _____ | _____ |
| cake | _____ | _____ |
| pickles | _____ | _____ |

WEEK 24
ACTIVITY 5
TOTAL /5

---

Name: _____

**Bonus Activity:** What is Round?

Look at the circles in each box. Imagine what they could be. Draw your ideas to make the circles into an object. Write the name of your object under your drawing.

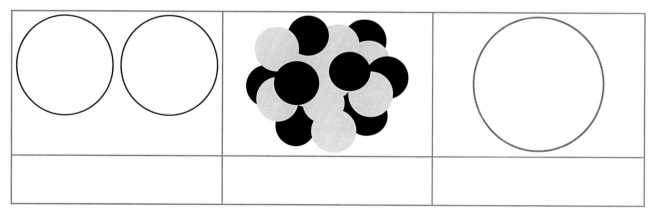

How do we know our Canadian flag is friendly? *It is always waving!*

MY CANADA

WEEK 24

Name: _____

**Fix these sentences.**

1. rosie dont wnt to plai withe me
   _____

2. well you halp me start a new gaim
   _____

**Circle the best word to fit in the sentence..**

3. My sister and (I, me) like to skip.
4. (We, Us) play skipping every day.

**Circle the word that comes first in ABC order.**

5. wolf     cat     skunk     bird

WEEK 25
ACTIVITY 1
TOTAL /5

---

Name: _____

**Fix these sentences.**

1. della gots no munny to spend
   _____

2. her cant buy no candy on saturday
   _____

**Circle the word that is spelled correctly.**

3. hurse     hawrse     horse     hourse

**Find the question. Circle it.**

4. Can you come to my house? Will be fun?
5. Colour is blue? What colour is your new hat?

WEEK 25
ACTIVITY 2
TOTAL /5

79

Name: _____

**Circle the best word.**

1. Grandpa likes to fish. (He, Him) always catches some big ones.
2. Can you help me catch worms? (Them, They) are really fast!

**Fix these sentences.**

3. me brother wont halp me fix this
   _____

4. i needs it fer sckool tomorrow
   _____

**Circle the word that doesn't belong.**

5. dog     cat     tiger     hamster

---

Name: _____

**Fix these sentences.**

1. gimme that toy, rite now
   _____

2. jack brung hims new trick to sckool
   _____

**Circle the word that matches the meaning.**

3. a thick string :     corn     core     cord     cork

**Question or Not a question?**

4. Over here beside me?          Question          Not a question
5. What time is it?               Question          Not a question

Name: _____

**Write the letter correctly on the lines below.**

dear holly
_____

do you want to go shopping on saturday
_____

my mom well tak us
_____

we cud go to the super dollar store
_____

yr friend, elsa
_____

WEEK 25
ACTIVITY 5
TOTAL /5

---

Name: _____

**Bonus Activity:** Up in the Trees

Some animals make their homes in trees. A bird's home is called a nest. The mother bird lays eggs in her nest. When the eggs hatch, she feeds her babies.

1. A bird's home is called

    (a) a den    (b) a nest    (c) a cage

2. The mother bird lays

    a) rocks    (b) leaves    (c) eggs

3. The mother bird feeds her

    (a) friends    (b) babies    (c) ants

WEEK 25

You could see *Bonhomme* at the Quebec Winter Carnival.

**MY CANADA**

Name: _____

**WEEK 26**

**ACTIVITY 1**

**TOTAL /5**

Circle the first word in ABC order.

1. Polly     Carson     Ted     Ben
2. sun       rain       wind    ice

Fix these sentences.

3. hims going to hals house
   _____

4. thay is going to build a tree fort
   _____

Write the correct word.

5. A baby chicken is called a _____

---

Name: _____

**ACTIVITY 2**

**TOTAL /5**

Same or opposite?

1. stop, go       Same     Opposite
2. grin, smile    Same     Opposite

How many syllables (word parts) do you hear?

3. elephant _____

Fix these sentences.

4. we runned around the yard too times
   _____

5. then we was tired and hote
   _____

82     SSR1144   ISBN: 9781771587303  © On The Mark Press

Name: _____

**Circle the pronoun that tells about the underlined words.**

1. <u>Katie and Ada</u> are my best friends.   She   They

2. The girls like to play <u>hopscotch.</u>   it   them

**Fix these sentences.**

3. has you ever ben to niagara falls
   _____

4. we is going there in july
   _____

**Where does this happen?**

5. We jumped on our sleds and down we went!  At the beach  On a big snowy hill

WEEK 26
ACTIVITY 3
TOTAL /5

---

Name: _____

**Fix these sentences.**

1. next sunday, im going to aunt mary's house
   _____

2. her live on hillwood street in markham, ontario
   _____

**Write the correct word on the line.**

3. Josie _____ to walk home.
          has / have

4. She will _____ to walk fast.
              has / have

**Circle the words that name birds.**

5. blue jay    frog    robin    woodpecker    fly

WEEK 26
ACTIVITY 4
TOTAL /5

Name: _____

# Combining Sentences

Write one good sentence using these short sentences.

1. Jim likes cookies. He likes chocolate chip cookies best.
   _____

2. My dog likes to run. My dog likes to play.
   _____

3. Cam is my friend. Cam is my best friend.
   _____

4. I have a new dress. My dress is green.
   _____

5. The baby smiled at me. The baby laughed at me.
   _____

**WEEK 26**
ACTIVITY 5
TOTAL /5

---

Name: _____

**Bonus Activity:** Six Silly Questions

Read the questions. Circle Yes or No.

1. Do puppies have wings?        Yes     No
2. Is the sun hot?               Yes     No
3. Can you read a book?          Yes     No
4. Do you smell with your ears?  Yes     No
5. Do you have three eyes?       Yes     No
6. Can you eat a peach?          Yes     No

**WEEK 26**

What is Canada's smallest bird? A hummingbird.

**MY CANADA**

Name: _____

**Fix these sentences.**

1. i red the story of <u>the three little pigs</u>
   _____

2. it ere funny but scary to
   _____

**Write the two words that make up each contraction.**

3. I'm _____ and _____

4. he's _____ and _____

**Circle two words that are opposites.**

5. fast    tall    slow    happy

**WEEK 27**
**ACTIVITY 1**
**TOTAL /5**

---

Name: _____

**Write the word that means more than one.**

1. one box    two _____

2. one dress    two _____

**Why did Jaxon start to cry? Underline your answer.**

3. Jaxon lost his money on the way home.

**Fix these sentences.**

4. this year, im gonna go to summer camp
   _____

5. has you ever went to hillwood camp before
   _____

**WEEK 27**
**ACTIVITY 2**
**TOTAL /5**

Name: _____

**WEEK 27**
**ACTIVITY 3**
**TOTAL /5**

**Write the best word on the line.**

1. Evan _____ the ball over the fence.
   hit / hitted

2. Eddie _____ fast to find it.
   runned / ran

**Fix these sentences.**

3. its fun to ran and ply at skool
   _____

4. we plays tag and ball evry daye
   _____

**Circle the words that tell about ducks.**

5. swim    quack    purple    fly

---

Name: _____

**WEEK 27**
**ACTIVITY 4**
**TOTAL /5**

**Write three words that rhyme with 'glow'**

1. glow: _____

**Fix these sentences.**

2. Them there strawberries is read
   _____

3. toni and me is going to luke for buggs
   _____

**Circle the words that name things.**

4. Many bees fly around our flowers.

5. Mother robin laid eggs in her nest.

Name: _____

**WEEK 27**

**ACTIVITY 5**

**TOTAL /5**

Real or Make-believe?

Read the sentence. Circle Real or Make-believe.

1. Crazy Cat flew in a red airplane.     Real     Make-believe
2. Rover ate the food in his dish.     Real     Make-believe
3. A shark likes to swim.     Real     Make-believe
4. The parrot sat reading his book.     Real     Make-believe
5. Boys and girls go to school.     Real     Make-believe

---

Name: _____

**WEEK 27**

**BONUS ACTIVITY**

**Bonus Activity:** Going Fishing

Find and circle the following words in the puzzle.

bass    perch    sunfish    pike    catfish    muskie    salmon

| s | a | l | m | o | n | q | q |
|---|---|---|---|---|---|---|---|
| m | u | s | k | i | e | w | h |
| a | q | n | a | q | r | e | c |
| c | w | z | f | i | b | d | r |
| g | e | c | d | i | a | x | e |
| c | a | t | f | i | s | h | p |
| t | h | v | f | l | s | h | t |
| e | k | i | p | r | a | j | j |

**MY CANADA**

Why doesn't a polar bear wear socks? It likes to go bear-foot!

Name: _____

**Put the apostrophe ( ' ) in the correct place**

1. Dales toy tractor
2. the boys skates

**Fix these sentences.**

3. i likes chocolate vanilla and strawberry ice creem
   _____

4. we took water cookies and sandwiches on the hike
   _____

**What will you need to paint a picture? Circle the words.**

5. paper    cookies    paints    water    candy

WEEK 28
ACTIVITY 1
TOTAL /5

---

Name: _____

**What is Mom making?**

1. Mom squeezed the lemons, added water and sugar, and stirred.
   _____

**Fix these sentences.**

2. debbie and me isnt going ovr their
   _____

3. carl mixed red purple and white paint
   _____

**Circle the rhyming words.**

4. cry    fly    baby    sky    party
5. fight    night    sign    might    right

WEEK 28
ACTIVITY 2
TOTAL /5

Name: _____

**WEEK 28 — ACTIVITY 3 — TOTAL /5**

**Circle the questions.**

1. Did the bird build a nest?   Eggs in the nest?
2. Come soon?   Can you come over?

**Circle the word that is spelled correctly.**

3. fathur    fauther    fother    father

**Fix the following sentences.**

4. whin wil you go to the movie
   _____

5. i is going tonight withe my sisiter, erin
   _____

---

Name: _____

**WEEK 28 — ACTIVITY 4 — TOTAL /5**

**Complete the sentence.**

1. A baby dog is called a _____

**Fix these sentences.**

2. jim founded this dim in the yard
   _____

3. him knowed it was frannys dime
   _____

**Circle the correct word in these sentences.**

4. The (gooses, geese) flew in a big V.
5. Harry's pet (mice, mouses) live in a cage.

Name: _____

**Putting Things Away**

Circle all the words that tell <u>where</u>.

1. Put your toys in the toy-box.
2. The books go on the bookshelf.
3. Hang your coat on the hook.
4. Put your slippers near your bed.
5. Put your crayons in the box.

WEEK 28
ACTIVITY 5
TOTAL /5

---

Name: _____

**Bonus Activity:** Scrambled Sentences

WEEK 28

Write these words in the right order to make a sentence.

On went party I Saturday to a
1. _____

birthday Gabby's It was
2. _____

hot dogs cake had and We
3. _____

fun! was It
4. _____

*Carvings on a totem pole tell the history of a family or a village.*

**MY CANADA**

Name: _____

**Fix these sentences.**

1. there were nothing in that olde box
   _____

2. rover runned and hided under the bed
   _____

**Circle the words that are spelled correctly.**

3. litel    littil    little    lettle

4. cood    cud    coude    could

**Write two words that rhyme with 'saw'**

5. _____

WEEK **29**

ACTIVITY **1**

TOTAL /5

---

Name: _____

**Correct these sentences.**

1. did her remember too take her too books to school
   _____

2. i wants too read the poem <u>alligator pie</u>
   _____

**Write the correct verb on the line.**

3. We all _____ for the singer.
   clap / clapping / clapped

4. Dad is _____ in the big race.
   run / running / ran

**Circle the word that needs an apostrophe.**

5. Marys    kiss    reads    washes

WEEK **29**

ACTIVITY **2**

TOTAL /5

Name: _____

**WEEK 29**

**Fix these sentences.**

1. my big brothr hitted the ball hard
   _____

2. isnt hims a gode ball player
   _____

**ACTIVITY 3**

**TOTAL /5**

**Circle the words that mean more than one.**

3. pig     cattle     kitten     geese
4. women     boy     children     man

**Real or Make-believe?**

5. The milk spilled on the floor.     Real     Make-believe

---

Name: _____

**WEEK 29**

**Circle the correct word for each sentence.**

1. Gina (don't, doesn't) like chocolate milk.
2. We (don't, doesn't) want to be late.

**Fix these sentences.**

3. my puppy, king, growed and growed
   _____

4. hims are to big to sleep on my bed
   _____

**ACTIVITY 4**

**татоL /5**

**How many syllables (word parts) do you hear?**

5. New Brunswick _____

92

Name: _____

## Sled Dogs

Read the story. Circle the right answer.

In Canada's North, dogs pull sleds over the snow. Dogsleds are better than cars or trucks in snow. The driver yells 'Mush!' and off they race.

**WEEK 29**

**ACTIVITY 5**

**TOTAL /5**

1. Sled dogs work   a) in the sea   b) in Canada's North   c) on a big hill
2. Dogs pull the sleds   a) over the sand   b) over the water   c) over the snow
3. Dogsleds are better than   a) boats   b) trucks or cars   c) bikes
4. The driver yells   a) Mush   b) Get going   c) Whoa
5. The dogs like to   a) walk   b) lie down   c) race

---

Name: _____

**Bonus Activity:** Work and Play at School!

Read these words that tell about <u>things to use</u> or <u>things to do</u> at school.

If the word names a thing, colour the box <u>yellow.</u>

If the word shows action, colour the box <u>blue</u>.

**WEEK 29**

| books | read | play | write |
|---|---|---|---|
| crayons | pencils | paper | run |
| desks | draw | scissors | markers |

**MY CANADA**  Beaver skins were used as money in early Canada.

Name: _____

**WEEK 30 — ACTIVITY 1 — TOTAL /5**

**Real or make-believe?**

1. A bear sleeps most of the winter.     Real     Make-believe

**Fix these sentences.**

2. helen were afraid of brents dog
   _____

3. sometime it bark a lots at childrun
   _____

**Circle the word that does not belong in the group.**

4. baseball     soccer     drawing     basketball

5. one     five     orange     ten     six

---

Name: _____

**WEEK 30 — ACTIVITY 2 — TOTAL /5**

**Same or opposite?**

1. start     stop     Same     Opposite

**Fix these sentences.**

2. cinderella weared a beautiful dres too the palace
   _____

3. she losed a glass slipper whin her runned away
   _____

**Write the number of syllables (word parts) you hear in each word.**

4. outside _____

5. understand _____

Name: _____

**Fix these sentences.**

1. i just lerned how to draw a dragin
   _____

2. now i is gonna draw a castel
   _____

**Circle the word that comes first in ABC order.**

3. Stella     Marie     Olive     Bree

**Circle the words that are spelled correctly.**

4. blahk     black     blawck     blak
5. thenk     thanck     thinck     thank

WEEK 30
ACTIVITY 3
TOTAL /5

---

Name: _____

**Fix these sentences.**

1. wee liked the song it's a small world
   _____

2. did you heared our class sanging it
   _____

**Unscramble the words to make a question.**

3. live     Where     you     do     _____

**Sentence or Not a sentence?.**

4. On my bike. I            Sentence     Not a sentence
5. Your new puppy is cute.  Sentence     Not a sentence

WEEK 30
ACTIVITY 4
TOTAL /5

Name: _____

**WEEK 30**
**ACTIVITY 5**
**TOTAL /5**

Circle the correct word.

1. Ivy and (I, me) went to the movie.

2. My aunt gave the picture to (I, me)

3. The baby (maked, made) a mess.

4. The boys (climbs, climbed) up the hill.

5. I (breaked, broke) my best toy.

---

Name: _____

**WEEK 30**

Bonus Activity: Read and Draw

Read the sentences. Draw a picture to show what the sentence is saying.

| | | |
|---|---|---|
| The wind was blowing. | Leaves fell from the trees. | Time for me to rake! |

**MY CANADA**

Why did the hockey player climb up a tree?
He wanted to play with the Maple Leafs!

Name: _____

**Circle the words that rhyme.**

1. big   bug   beg   rug   hug
2. bet   bat   get   met   but

**Fix these sentences.**

3. well you call mr drake fer me
   _____

4. i needs to aske hims about my homework
   _____

**Put in the commas.**

5. Tuesday May 2  2017

WEEK **31**

ACTIVITY **1**

TOTAL /5

---

Name: _____

**Write the two words that make each compound word.**

1. into _____ and _____
2. upstairs _____ and _____

**Fix these sentences.**

3. Karens bike are read and blew
   _____

4. im not gonna go to the gaim
   _____

**Circle the correct word.**

5. Janet put on her raincoat and boots. Was it …… sunny? OR rainy?

WEEK **31**

ACTIVITY **2**

TOTAL /5

Name: _____

**WEEK 31**
**ACTIVITY 3**
**TOTAL /5**

Circle the correct word.

1. Kim and I walked (to, two, too) the playground.
2. Her little brother wanted to come (to, two, too).

How many syllables (word parts) do you hear?

3. grandmother _____

Fix these sentences.

4. robert munsch write funny buks
   _____

5. whut are your favourite buk to red
   _____

---

Name: _____

**WEEK 31**
**ACTIVITY 4**
**TOTAL /5**

What will happen next?

1. Dad turned on the television. Then ..... he went outside. OR he sat down to watch it.

Fix these sentences.

2. i didnt see no apples in that there tree
   _____

3. is you trying to play a track on me
   _____

Question or Not a question?

4. Does Chloe have a new pet?    Question    Not a question
5. The best score?                Question    Not a question

Name: _____

**Rhyming Riddles**

Use these words to answer the riddles: four, dog, yellow, candy, ball

1. I am a pet. I rhyme with 'log' _____

2. I am a colour. I rhyme with 'fellow' _____

3. I am a toy. I rhyme with 'hall' _____

4. I am a treat. I rhyme with 'dandy'. _____

5. I am a number. I rhyme with 'door'. _____

WEEK 31
ACTIVITY 5
TOTAL /5

---

Name: _____

**Bonus Activity:** The message is _____ under the boxes.

Colour the boxes with the letters X, Y, and Z green. Read the words that are left. Write the message.

| I | X | l | i | k | e | Y | t | o | Z |
|---|---|---|---|---|---|---|---|---|---|
| p | l | a | y | X | w | i | t | h | Y |
| m | y | Z | f | r | i | e | n | d | s. |

_____

_____

WEEK 31

**MY CANADA**

Which bears like playing in the rain? Drizzly bears!

Name: _____

**Fix these sentences.**

1. me and lee wants to plai at lukes house
   _____

2. him askt us to cum over on friday
   _____

**Circle the words that rhyme with 'down'**

3. brown   door   town   den   frown

**Same or opposite?**

4. inside, outside        Same        Opposite
5. big, huge              Same        Opposite

WEEK
**32**

ACTIVITY
**1**

TOTAL
**/5**

---

Name: _____

**What time of year might this take place?**

1. The plants begin to grow.    Winter    Spring    Summer    Fall

**Fix these sentences.**

2. wher does you and your famly live
   _____

3. i lives in the green horse on elm street
   _____

**Real or Make-believe?**

4. The dragon breathed fire at us.    Real    Make-believe
5. Apples grow on trees.              Real    Make-believe

WEEK
**32**

ACTIVITY
**2**

TOTAL
**/5**

Name: _____

**WEEK 32 — ACTIVITY 3 — TOTAL /5**

**Sentence or Not a sentence?**

1. Under the bed.        Sentence        Not a sentence
2. Come home early.      Sentence        Not a sentence

**Fix these sentences.**

3. brish your tooths and comb your haire

_____

4. which shoese should i wear to bonnies party

_____

**Put in the commas.**

5. Sunday August 25 1974

---

Name: _____

**WEEK 32 — ACTIVITY 4 — TOTAL /5**

**Circle the word that means more than one 'church'.**

1. churchs        churchis        churches        churchees

**Fix these sentences.**

2. ms green wnts all the boys to halp her

_____

3. how longe will all them jobs take

_____

**Circle the correct word.**

4. (She, Her) can't reach the doll.
5. Will you please help (she, her)?

Name: _____

**Picture Clues**

Look at the picture clues. Finish the sentence with the correct word.

1. You can eat an _____.
2. You can tie your _____.
3. You can read a _____.
4. You can fly a _____.
5. You can sleep in a _____.

WEEK **32**

ACTIVITY **5**

TOTAL **/5**

---

Name: _____

**Bonus Activity:** A Not – So – Secret Message!

Find the message by writing the letters in the boxes.

Write the letter that comes <u>before</u> each one you see.

The first one has been done to help you.

| C |   |   |   |   |   |   |   |   |   |   |   |   | ! |
|---|---|---|---|---|---|---|---|---|---|---|---|---|---|
| d | b | o | b | e | b | j | t | u | i | f | c | f | t | u | ! |

WEEK **32**

BONUS ACTIVITY

*Anne of Green Gables is a famous Canadian book.*

**MY CANADA**

# ANSWER KEY

### WEEK 1: ACTIVITY 1

1. Come here, please.     Sentence
2. Over there.            Not a sentence
3. trees
4. boys
5. My kitten is named Puff.

### WEEK 1: ACTIVITY 2

1. The dog barks.
2. The bell rings.
3. I walk to school.
5. an : can, Dan, man, Nan, pan, tan, van

### WEEK 1: ACTIVITY 3

1. Will you come to my house?
2. did not : didn't
3. it is : it's
4. - ook : cook, book, look
5. - at : bat, cat, mat, pat

### WEEK 1: ACTIVITY 4

1. It snowed all day.             Yes
2. Our snowman can dance.         No
3. I play basketball on Wednesday.
4. boy      bed
5. not      now

### WEEK 1: ACTIVITY 5

1. Do you like chocolate ice cream ?   *
2. I like to play tag .
3. I am a fast runner .
4. What games do you like ?   *
5. Let's go to the park .

### BONUS ACTIVITY: ON MY TABLE, I CAN SEE .....

| c | u | p | f | o | r | k |
|---|---|---|---|---|---|---|
|   |   | l |   |   |   | n |
| g | l | a | s | s |   | i |
|   |   | t |   | p |   | f |
|   |   | e |   | o |   | e |
|   |   |   |   | o |   |   |
|   |   |   |   | n |   |   |

### WEEK 2: ACTIVITY 1

1. Is he your friend?
2. Where does he live?
3. out side : outside
4. cow boy : cowboy
5. Name of today ... written with a capital letter.

### WEEK 2 ACTIVITY 2

1. At home.                    Not a sentence
2. Feed the dog, please.       Sentence
3. The cat ran after the mouse.  Real
4. Danny ate the cake.
5. He loves cake.

### WEEK 2 ACTIVITY 3

1. tell    well
2. Let's go to the pond.
3. We might see a frog.
4. look
5. coat

## Week 2 Activity 4

1. Mary has a new puppy.
2. What does she call it?
3. ick : lick, pick, trick
4. Sam (eats) his lunch.
5. He (walks) to school.

## Week 2 Activity 5

| eggs   | shoes    | red      | juice    |
|--------|----------|----------|----------|
| toast  | (candy)  | blue     | water    |
| (crow) | boots    | green    | (bread)  |
| jam    | socks    | (pencil) | milk     |

## Bonus Activity: Letter Partners

| M n | G g | T t |
|-----|-----|-----|
| P p | L i | S s |
| B d | H h | W v |

## Week 3 Activity 1

1. These kittens do funny tricks.
2. They like to jump and play.
3. sun    run
4. man    pan
5. one : 1    four : 4

## Week 3 Activity 2

1. A long way to go.                    Not a sentence
2. It is a sunny day.                    Sentence
3. Randy wasn't at school today.
4. Was he sick?
5. A baby bird fell out of its nest.    Yes

## Week 3 Activity 3

1. The light turned green so..... I walked across the street
2. The teacher began to read so ..... we listened
3. My birthday is in July.
4. I will be seven years old.
5. all: ball, call, fall, tall small

## Week 3 Activity 4

1. I can jump rope.
2. Anna gave her rope to me.
3. I live in Calgary.
4. It is a great city.
5. work

## Week 3: Activity 5    Matching Contractions

Word pairs:   are not   were not   have not   was not   did not

Contractions:   aren't   weren't   haven't   wasn't   didn't

## Bonus Activity: I Love Shopping!

1. Mom took me shopping.
2. We went shopping on Saturday.
3. I got new shoes, a jacket and a game.

## Week 4 Activity 1

1. Did he find his socks?
2. They were on the floor in his bedroom.
3. came
4. beaver   2
5. Halifax   3

## Week 4 Activity 2

1. huge
2. This is the (girl's) hat.
3. The little (boy's) toy was broken..
4. Will you come to my party?
5. Did your dad get a new car?

## Week 4 Activity 3

1. up:    down
2. little:    big
3. Tony and Teddy read well.
4. They like animal stories.
5. - ang: bang, rang, sang

## Week 4 Activity 4

1. Bob      Dave      Mike
2. Rory     Sally     Tanya
3. We will sing with Ms Jones.
4. Let's try 'Small World'.
5. girls    cats      toys

## Week 4 Activity 5

| Picture showing a three-ball snowman – no eyes, etc. | Picture showing child rolling a big snowball | Picture showing a finished snowman – eyes, nose, mouth, hat |
|---|---|---|
| Number 2 | Number 1 | Number 3 |

Sentence 1, 2, 3 answers will vary.

## Bonus Activity: Fairy Tale Folks

|   | Clue |   |   |   |   |   |   |   |
|---|---|---|---|---|---|---|---|---|
| 1 | I am the man who wears the crown. | k | i | n | g | * | * | * |
| 2 | I am the woman who wears the crown. | q | u | e | e | n | * | * |
| 3 | I am the evil person. | w | i | t | c | h | * | * |
| 4 | I am the boy child of the king and queen. | p | r | i | n | c | e | * |
| 5 | I am the girl child of the king and queen | p | r | i | n | c | e | s | s |

## Week 5 Activity 1

1. boxes
2. Did you read this book?
3. I like to read joke books.
4. at: bat, cat, fat, mat
5. ell: bell, fell, tell, well

## Week 5 Activity 2

1. You can draw a fish.              Real
2. Franny lives on the moon.         Make-believe
3. Penny will come to the show.
4. Pat can't go with us.
5. The wind blew hard, so … the leaves fell.

## Week 5 Activity 3

1. We went to the game.
2. Mom made us some cookies.
3. 1 get      3 mat      2 hut
4. I go to Gordon Scott Public School.
5. There are eleven classrooms and thirteen teachers.

## Week 5 Activity 4

1. Alberta 3
2. We like to play baseball.
3. John is the best batter.

Complete the sentences with the best word.
4. The bees buzzed around the hive.
5. Ms Carson read a good story to the class.

## Week 5: Activity 5   Word and Shape Match

Check for accurate picture and word match.

## Bonus Activity: Compound Words Riddles

1. What am I? cupcake      My picture _____
2. What am I? ladybug      My picture _____

## Week 6 Activity 1

1. Did she open the door?
2. I will help you clean your room.
3. I (am) going away on Sunday.
4. We (are) going shopping.
5. that's: that is

## Week 6 Activity 2

1. hog: dog, fog, log
2. Can a fish read a book?      No
3. Can a boy wear a hat?        Yes
4. Mice like to eat cheese.
5. They like cookies too.

## Week 6 Activity 3

1. pigs
2. The girls (are) playing in the yard.
3. She (is) going to help her mom.
4. Finn can't go with us.
5. Are you leaving early in the morning?

## Week 6 Activity 4

1. Do you have any new games?
2. This game is the best one.
3. Stayed at home.           Not a sentence
4. My mom is picking me up.   Sentence
5. school

## Week 6 Activity 5

1. Let's go play tag.
2. I ate my lunch.
3. Please help me.
4. Dolly fed her cat.
5. Susie made some popcorn.

## Bonus Activity:   Following Directions

Check for accuracy of details in drawing.

## Week 7 Activity 1

1. Cinderella wore glass slippers.
2. She lost one when she was running away.
3. That (was) a funny joke.
4. Everyone (is) still laughing.
5. A snowman might melt in the sun.     Real

## Week 7 Activity 2

1. slow: fast
2. sad: happy
3. ap: cap, lap, map, nap
4. Will you come withe me to the store?
5. We can get some ice cream.

## Week 7 Activity 3

1. rock
2. Let's gets pizza from Pizza Hut.
3. Will Dad take us to pick it up?
4. Woodstock 2
5. Wonderland 3

## Week 7 Activity 4

1. Ms Hunter read us the story, Dandelion.
2. It was about a lion trying to fix his hair.
3. trees      branches      nests
4. Anna
5. Josh

## Week 7 Activity 5

1. We plant seeds in the garden … in the spring
2. Jill made a snow fort … in the winter
3. We go swimming at the beach … in the summer
4. Our grass starts to grow …. in the spring
5. Leaves fall from the trees … in the fall

## Bonus Activity:   Crack the Code

| 9 | 12 | 15 | 22 | 5 | 3 | 1 | 14 | 1 | 4 | 1 |   |
|---|----|----|----|---|---|---|----|---|---|---|---|
| I | l  | o  | v  | e | C | a | n  | a | d | a | ! |

## Week 8 Activity 1

1. My grandpa lives on a farm.
2. He has cows, pigs and chickens.
3. My brother loves cookies.    Yes
4. Chocolate cookies.           No
5. go: no, so

## Week 8 Activity 2

1. We walk (to) school each day.
2. I have (two) friends with me.
3. stop
4. When will Freddy get here.
5. My kitten, Mitten, has two black feet.

### Week 8 Activity 3

1. Ms White is kind and (she) is a good teacher.
2. Mr. Earl sings and (he) plays the piano.
3. Little Red Riding Hood walked in the woods
4. Do you think she was afraid?
5. can't: can not

### Week 8 Activity 4

1. A bird is building a nest in our tree.
2. Do you think it will lay eggs there?
3. That's the biggest puddle in our yard.
4. Jake put on his jacket and then ...... he will go outside
5. The sky looked black and then ... it started to rain

### Week 8 Activity 5

1. Chocolate is my favourite ice cream.
2. Those black lab puppies are cute.
3. My birthday party is on Saturday.
4. We played a game of ball in the backyard.
5. Aunt Jane is coming tomorrow from Moncton.

### Bonus Activity:   Find the People Words

| mother | fireman | aunt    | grandma |
|--------|---------|---------|---------|
| tree   | rock    | uncle   | house   |
| dog    | father  | grandpa | car     |
| baker  | kitten  | horse   | cowboy  |

### Week 9 Activity 1

1. hot: cold
2. short: tall
3. I want to go to Toronto.
4. I want to see a Blue Jays game.
5. cook     cold

### Week 9 Activity 2

1. boy: boys
2. box: boxes
3. It is cold at the North Pole.     Real
4. Let's go to the lake.
5. Do you like to swim at the beach?

### Week 9 Activity 3

1. Can a snowman dance?     No
2. What colour is your new puppy?
3. Mine is brown and white?
4. sun     shine : sunshine
5. in     side: inside

### Week 9 Activity 4

1. Christmas day is in December.
2. Family Day is in February.
3. Billy put milk in a glass. Then ...... he will drink it.
4. Our team (has) played a good game.
5. We (have) two new players.

### Week 9 Activity 5

| Things to Eat | Things to Wear |
|---------------|----------------|
| apples        | coat           |
| bread         | hat            |
| eggs          | shirt          |
| meat          | shoes          |

### Bonus Activity:   At the Beach

Check drawing for accuracy of details.

### Week 10 Activity 1

1. - ad: bad, fad, had, lad, mad
2. - et: bet, get, met, net, jet
3. Today is a sunny day.
4. Do you want to play at the park?
5. get

### Week 10 Activity 2

1. (I) need a new pair of boots.
2. Mom will buy (me) some on Saturday.
3. apple
4. My grandma lives in England.
5. I am going to see her in July.

### Week 10 Activity 3

1. dog
2. cats like to chase mice.
3. My cat, Flash, hunts in our yard.
4. Summer is in July.     Yes
5. Winter is in August.    No

### Week 10 Activity 4

1. Are you going to see the movie?
2. We are going on Friday night.
3. man    fan    pan
4. How long is the story     Yes
5. I want to go home    No

### Week 10 Activity 5

1. Cats and dogs have fur.
2. I like baseball and soccer.
3. I have a sister and a brother.
4. Dan and Ann are my friends.
5. Sue likes apples and grapes.

### Bonus Activity: Outdoor Fun

|   | h |   |   | r | u | n |   |
| f | i | s | h |   |   | c |   |
|   | k |   |   | p | l | a | y |
|   | e |   | s | w | i | m |   |
|   |   |   | a |   |   | p |   |
|   |   | b | i | k | e |   |   |
|   |   |   | l |   |   |   |   |

### Week 11 Activity 1

1. I don't want to play soccer.
2. Can Patti and Ali come over tonight?
3. cook    took    look
4. shook    crook
5. Dan is coming to my house to play.

### Week 11 Activity 2

1. Rained all day    Not a sentence
2. We saw a rainbow in the sky    Sentence
3. The Grinch is a Christmas story.
4. Grandma Smith is coming on Sunday.
5. Beavers lay eggs.    Make-believe

### Week 11 Activity 3

1. Do you hide eggs for Easter?
2. I like hunting for them.
3. (Two) boys ran down the street.
4. They live next door (to) me.
5. That puppy is the smallest one.

### Week 11 Activity 4

1. Canada geese fly south.    Real
2. Canada geese lay golden eggs.    Make-believe
3. I have a little brother named Bobby.
4. He is two years old.
5. We (painted) the fence.

### Week 11 Activity 5

**Growing a Pumpkin**
**Number the sentences in the correct order.**
2 Plant a pumpkin seed in the ground.
1 Dig a small hole in the ground.
4 Water the ground where the seed is.
3 Cover the seed with dirt.
5 Wait for the pumpkin plant to grow.

### Bonus Activity: Action Words

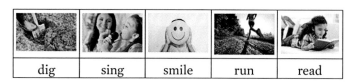

| dig | sing | smile | run | read |

## Week 12 Activity 1

1. There are robin eggs in the nest.      Sentence
2. Monday morning Jen will go to school.
3. She is in Grade One.
4. feet:   beet    meet    greet
5. blow:   grow    snow    flow

## Week 12 Activity 2

1. I can ride a bike.
2. I hope I get a new one soon.
3. they
4. went
5. The elephant is the (biggest) animal in the zoo.

## Week 12 Activity 3

1. My dog Cleo had four puppies.
2. I want to keep the black one.
3. Fluffy is playing with a toy mouse. Is Fluffy ..... a cat?
4. We are wet. We are at the beach. Are we .... swimming?
5. (i) am going to (t)oronto on (m)onday.

## Week 12 Activity 4

1. Remembrance Day is November 11.
2. We think about our Canadian soldiers.
3. Montreal 3
4. Ottawa 3
5. 3 carrot   1 apple   2 banana   4 date

## Week 12 Activity 5

1. The girls began to sing (loudly).
2. The man was in a (hurry).
3. The mouse ran away (quickly).
4. Hank told his story (sadly).
5. Annie smiled (happily) when she won.

## Bonus Activity: Compound Words

| outside | movie  | sunshine |
| ------- | ------ | -------- |
| puppy   | inside | fort     |
| today   | castle | football |

## Week 13 Activity 1

1. quick
2. Does he like chocolate cake?
3. January is a very cold month.
4. If it rains, the ground is wet.      Yes
5. A car can drive to the moon.      No

## Week 13 Activity 2

1. won't: will not
2. they'll: they will/shall
3. Does Mary like to shop in Regina?
4. Yes, she goes with her sister, Lizzie.
5. My brother is taller than me.

## Week 13 Activity 3

1. Sally has long brown hair.    b) what grows on your head
2. Have you read the story <u>Hop</u> on <u>Pop</u>?
3. I like the book, <u>Red Fish</u>, <u>Blue Fish</u>.
4. bump    dump    lump
5. ten    red    bed

## Week 13 Activity 4

1. ball
2. What do you eat on thanksgiving?
3. Christmas is in December.
4. The little kittens lost their mittens.   Make-believe
5. The bird flew high in the sky.      Real

## Week 13 Activity 5

| Green Things | Red Things   |
| ------------ | ------------ |
| grass        | strawberries |
| lime         | cherries     |
| plant        | stop sign    |

## Bonus Activity: Vowel Maze

START

| a | n | u | e | o | w | q |
|---|---|---|---|---|---|---|
| e | o | i | p | a | u | i |
| d | m | z | h | t | k | a |

FINISH

## Bonus Activity: 'ch' Word Scramble

| Picture of a chair | Picture of a cherry | Picture of a piece of cheese | Picture of a chick | Picture of a chain |
|---|---|---|---|---|
| arihc | rrhcey | eeches | kcihc | nihac |
| chair | cherry | cheese | chick | chain |

### Week 14 Activity 1

1. Monday is the first school day of the week.
2. On Sunday we are going to see Grandma.
3. buffalo     3
4. one baby         two   babies
5. one fox          two   foxes

### Week 15 Activity 1

1. cab:    dab    crab    slab
2. ring:   sing   bring   zing
3. Mon.
4. I made a jack-o-lantern for Hallowe'en.
5. Did it have a scary face?

### Week 14 Activity 2

1. The best day of the week is Saturday.
2. What do you like to do on Saturday?
3. My mom is busy.     (She) is making lunch.
4. Our family is big.     (It) has seven people.
5. Beavers are good swimmers.          True

### Week 15 Activity 2

1. The truck zoomed down the road.   Sentence
2. Today we are going to the dentist.
3. My sister, Lily, doesn't want to go.
Circle the word that is spelled correctly.
4. purple
5. green

### Week 14 Activity 3

1. The tiny mouse ran under the bed.    Real
2. 'You can't catch me!' the mouse called.   Make-believe
3. We clapped at the end of the show.
4. It was about a lost princess named Esmai.
5. cold     hot     opposite

### Week 15 Activity 3

1. Is an ant small?        Yes
2. Mr. Brown is my teacher.    (He) reads us good stories.
3. Mom made our lunch.        (She) is a good cook.
4. What day is Tony's party?
5. I think it is on Friday.

### Week 14 Activity 4

1. I love to swim at the beach.
2. We are going there on Friday.
3. The dog is barking.      It
4. My dad will tell it to stop.     He
5. What a big herd of cattle!     A group, bunch

### Week 15 Activity 4

1. Mom lit the candles.
2. The starter yelled 'GO!'
3. Will you come to the library with me?
4. I am looking for a book called <u>Knock</u>, <u>Knock Jokes</u>.
5. Halifax:    3

### Week 14 Activity 5    What Goes ........?

1. Drip, drip:  water tap
2. Toot, toot: a horn
3. Buzz, buzz: bee
4. Boom, boom: drum
5. Ring, ring: telephone

### Week 15 Activity 5

| Living Things | Non-living Things |
|---|---|
| flower | bike |
| father | shovel |
| cat | ball |

## Bonus Activity: I See Red!

|   |   |   |   | c |   |   |   |
|---|---|---|---|---|---|---|---|
| s | p | a | g | h | e | t | t | i |
|   | l | p |   | e |   | o |   |   |
|   | u | p |   | r |   | m | a | j |
|   | m | l |   | r | a |   |   | e |
|   |   | e |   | y |   | t |   | l |
| l | o | l | l | i | p | o | p | l |
|   |   |   |   |   |   |   |   | o |

### Week 16 Activity 1

1. We sat quietly as Ms Gray began to speak. Classroom
2. Sally got a new coat. (She) picked a red one.
3. Tommy's new puppy is all black. (It) is very cute.
4. My new bike is red and black.
5. I got it for my birthday on Saturday.

### Week 16 Activity 2

1. The elephant danced along the street.  Make-believe
2. find:  kind   mind
3. that:  bat    mat
4. I play baseball on Monday and Thursday.
5. Would you like to join our team?

### Week 16 Activity 3

1. night: day
2. hot: cold
3. A   L   R   C   T
4. Penny's new mittens are missing.
5. Let's help her look for them.

### Week 16 Activity 4

1. Dad left for work early today.
2. Brush your teeth before you go to bed.
3. Mom called my name. So ...... I answered her.
4. Dan lost his pencil. So ...... He looked for it.
5. toy

### Week 16 Activity 5

1. Amy
2. Cara
3. Donnie
4. Fanny
5. Gary
6. Logan

## Bonus Activity: Looking for Shapes

Check for accuracy of shape identification and colours.

### Week 17 Activity 1

1. Dad lost his keys on Sunday.
2. Where are you going today?
3. canada     toronto
4. susie      alice
5. bent   cent   lent   rent   sent

### Week 17 Activity 2

1. fox    kittens    beaver.
2. Did you get a letter in the mail?
3. Grandma sends us a card on our birthday.
4. Jill's dolls
5. Timmy's toys

### Week 17 Activity 3

1. (You and I) can go to the movies.
2. (He and she) play baseball on my team.
3. this
4. Will you please hand me the book?
5. I'll bring it to you now.

### Week 17 Activity 4

1. The cow jumped over the moon.    Make-believe
2. The farmer milks his cows.    Real
3. Grandma got a new sun hat.
4. It is red, blue, and yellow.
5. little: tiny small wee

### Week 17 Activity 5    Cause and Effect

1. If you step in the puddle ................your shoes will get wet.
2. If you run fast ....................you will win the race.
3. If you don't don't feed your puppy......it will whine.
4. If you play our game ....................you will have fun.
5. If you help your Mom ....................she will be happy.

### Bonus Activity:    Colour Code

1. blue
2. red
3. yellow

### Week 18 Activity 1

1. Alex was sick yesterday.
2. He feels better today.
3. Did Theo get a new toy?
4. He wants a red firetruck.
5. We play (baseball) and (basketball).

### Week 18 Activity 2

1. (t)he twins are (t)im and (t)om.
2. (t)hey live on (o)ak (s)treet.
3. Sandy's favourite colour is blue.
4. What will you do this weekend?
5. The last day of school        Not a sentence

### Week 18 Activity 3

1. Mike and his dad are going to Toronto.
2. They are going to a Blue Jays ball game.
3. Saturday 3
4. sunshine 2
5. day    play    say

### Week 18 Activity 4

1. 4 soon    2 den    3 hunt    1 bug
2. I saw a robin yesterday.
3. It was building a nest in our big tree.
4. isn't: is and not
5. don't: do and not

### Week 18 Activity 5

4 The bird found some string.
2 The bird looked for a good place for a nest.
1 The bird flew up into our big tree.
3 The bird flew down.
5 The bird is building a nest

### Bonus Activity:    Read, Draw and Colour

Check for accuracy of sentence/picture match.

### Week 19 Activity 1

1. This is a good book.
2. It is called <u>Danny and the Dinosaurs</u>.
3. Jump in and make a big splash! Jumping into water/pool
4. We went to their house.
5. Go stand over there.

### Week 19 Activity 2

1. time
2. Tami sang a good song.
3. We all clapped and clapped for her.
4. apple    grapes    banana
5. kittens    puppies    lambs

### Week 19 Activity 3

1. quacks    swims    flies
2. We took the cookies.
3. Will you take this dish, please?
4. Come with me to see the chicks.
5. Aren't they fluffy little birds?

### Week 19 Activity 4

1. 'Brush your teeth before you go to bed'    Mom, Dad
2. 'Listen carefully, class'    Teacher
3. does
4. Our team is called the Red Runners.
5. We wear red hats and red shirts.

## Week 19 Activity 5

Miss Sophie Greene
5 Pine Street
Kingston, Ontario.

### Bonus Activity: Tell Me the Time

Check clock for accuracy according to instructions.

## Week 20 Activity 1

1. Jack runs like a deer.     Runs very fast
2. playground: play and ground
3. beehive: bee and hive
4. My friends and I went to see Frozen.
5. We liked Elsa and Olaf the best.

## Week 20 Activity 2

1. Let's go skating on Sunday.
2. Will you please call Dana for me?
3. bobsled 2
4. tennis 2
5. St.

## Week 20 Activity 3

1. go: come
2. I like to play with my friend, Jeff.
3. He is a nice boy and is funny.
4. I filled my glass with milk. Then …… I drank it.
5. The toast popped up. Then …… I buttered it.

## Week 20 Activity 4

1. Kayla
2. Abe
3. Mr. and Mrs. Lee live next door.
4. How long have they lived there?
5. carrots    dog

## Week 20 Activity 5

1. Wear your raincoat and you won't get wet.
2. We give sunflower seeds to the birds.
3. Take a flashlight so you can see in the dark.
4. I had a big pancake for breakfast.
5. My uncle is a cowboy on a ranch.

### Bonus Activity: Your Story

Check for accuracy of picture/sentence match.

## Week 21 Activity 1

1. Hot dogs for lunch          Not a Sentence
2. I love chocolate milk!      Sentence
3. Let's watch a movie on TV.
4. Do you want some popcorn?
5. mr     dr     mrs

## Week 21 Activity 2

1. Judy drew a good picture.
2. It was a rainbow in the sky.
3. dip: chip, lip, nip, hip,
4. out: bout, pout, shout
5. We are buying apples, bread and milk.
   Supermarket, grocery store

## Week 21 Activity 3

1. plays     jumps     licks
2. I got a letter from Sarah.
3. She lives in Calgary, Alberta.
4. I made a snowman in the summer.    Make-believe
5. Apples are good for you to eat.    Real

## Week 21 Activity 4

1. Uncle Fred is the best uncle.
2. He takes me go-cart racing.
3. We (were) all going out to play.
4. Marty (was) 'It' for tag.
5. boxes

## Week 21 Activity 5 Canada Quiz

1. Canada's flag is red and green.      No
2. Canada has three seasons.            No
3. Polar bears live in Canada.          Yes
4. Beavers live in Canada.              Yes
5. Mounties are police officers.        Yes

### Bonus Activity: 'Bl' Blends

| Clue | | | | | |
|---|---|---|---|---|---|
| 1. I am the colour of the sky. | b | l | u | e | * |
| 2. The wind does this. | b | l | o | w | * |
| 3. I am flames or a fire. | b | l | a | z | e |
| 4. The opposite of 'white'. | b | l | a | c | k |
| 5. Not able to see. | b | l | i | n | d |

### Week 22 Activity 1

1. teeth
2. men
3. bush
4. The girls have read the poem 'Anna Banana'
5. They say it when they are skipping.

### Week 22 Activity 2

1. terrible 3
2. from
3. about
4. Jon can do it better.
5. We want to go to the park on Sunday.

### Week 22 Activity 3

1. Mom gave me a loonie for helping. So ...... I will put it in my bank.
2. I put on my boots and raincoat. So ..... It must be raining.
3. blue    yellow    orange
4. I go to Hill Park School
5. It is on Maple Street on Windsor, Ontario.

### Week 22 Activity 4

1. He blows a whistle to stop the game.    Referee
2. Will Patty come to Betty's party?
3. She plans to come if her mom lets her.
4. Sam doesn't have (any) money.
5. (No) treats for him today!

### Week 22 Activity 5

1. mother
2. father
3. sister
4. uncle
5. aunt

### Bonus Activity: Things I Like to Do

Answers will vary.

### Week 23 Activity 1

1. Could you help the new boy with his books?
2. He needs a friend to play with too.
3. The sky is falling!  Make-believe
4. Bobby has his toys with him.
5. Annie plays with her dolls.

### Week 23 Activity 2

1. Will you look for the ball I lost?
2. It is red and blue with yellow stars.
3. My (sister) and (brother) are watching a movie.
4. (Chris) and (Hank) like to play ball.
5. let us: let's

### Week 23 Activity 3

1. Chad and I can't go to the show.
2. Have you seen the movie, <u>Boss Baby</u>?
3. black    white
4. The boy climbed to the top of the tree.    Real
5. Jack climbed to the top of the beanstalk.    Make-believe

### Week 23 Activity 4

1. school
2. one party    two  parties
3. one leaf    two  leaves
4. Jane won the most ribbons for running.
5. Is she the fastest girl in your class?

## WEEK 23 ACTIVITY 5

2 It began to rain and rain.
3 The rain stopped.
1 The sky was full of dark clouds.
5 I saw a rainbow in the sky.
4 I looked out the window.

### BONUS ACTIVITY: HOMONYM WORD SEARCH

| b | e | e |   | w | e | e | k |
|---|---|---|---|---|---|---|---|
| l | t |   | m | b |   |   | t |
| u | w | b | e | a | r |   | o |
| e | o | b | a | r | e | n | o |
|   |   |   | t | e |   |   |   |
|   |   | t | o |   | b | i | e | w |
| w | e | a | k |   |   |   |   |
|   |   | e |   |   |   |   |   |
|   |   | m |   |   | w | o | n |

## WEEK 24 ACTIVITY 1

1. Dad stopped because the light turned red.
2. Abi ran the fastest of all the girls.
3. Did she win every race?
4. Out in the backyard.          Not a sentence
5. We like to play tag.          Sentence

## WEEK 24 ACTIVITY 2

1. feet
2. wives.
3. Pete is my best friend.
4. Tell us all about your game.
5. bee    see    wee

## WEEK 24 ACTIVITY 3

1. Tommy climbed the big tree.    Real
2. I rode my bike to Larry's house.
3. Does he live very far away?
4. Mom took out her cookie cookbook. So … She is going to bake cookies.
5. Sally writes a note on a card to her Grandma. So ….. She will mail it.

## WEEK 24 ACTIVITY 4

1. We have gone to all the soccer games.
2. We cheer each time our team scores.
3. Monday:    Mon.
4. October:    Oct.
5. There are pigs, cows and horses on Grandpa's farm.

## WEEK 24 ACTIVITY 5

Sweet Things          Sour Things
sugar                 lemons
candy                 grapefruit
cake                  pickles

### BONUS ACTIVITY: WHAT IS ROUND?

Answers will vary.

## WEEK 25 ACTIVITY 1

1. Rosie doesn't want to play with me.
2. Will you help me start a new game?
3. My sister and (I) like to skip.
4. (We) play skipping every day.
5. bird

## WEEK 25 ACTIVITY 2

1. Della has no money to spend.
2. She can't buy any candy on Saturday.
3. horse
4. Can you come to my house?
5. What colour is your new hat?

## WEEK 25 ACTIVITY 3

1. Grandpa likes to fish.   (He) always catches some big ones.
2. Can you help me catch worms? (They) are really fast!
3. My brother won't help me fix this.
4. I need it for school tomorrow.
5. tiger

## Week 25 Activity 4

1. Give me that toy, right now.
2. Jack brought his new truck to school.
3. a thick string: cord
4. Over here beside me?     Not a question
5. What time is it?     Question

## Week 25 Activity 5

Dear Holly

Do you want to go shopping on Saturday?

My mom will take us.

We could go to the Super Dollar Store.

Your friend, Elsa

## Bonus Activity: Up in the Trees

1. A bird's home is called     b) a nest
2. The mother bird lays     c) eggs
3. The mother bird feeds her     b) babies

## Week 26 Activity 1

1. Ben
2. ice
3. He is going to Hal's house.
4. They are going to build a tree fort.
5. A baby chicken is called a chick.

## Week 26 Activity 2

1. stop   go     Opposite
2. grin   smile     Same
3. elephant 3
4. We ran around the yard two times.
5. Then we were tired and hot.

## Week 26 Activity 3

1. <u>Katie</u> and <u>Ada</u> are my best friends.     They
2. The girls like to play <u>hopscotch</u>.     it
3. Have you ever been to Niagara Falls?
4. We are going there in July.
5. We jumped on our sleds and down we went! On a big snowy hill

## Week 26 Activity 4

1. Next Sunday, I'm going to Aunt Mary's house.
2. She lives on Hillwood Street in Markham, Ontario
3. Josie has to walk home.
4. She will have to walk fast.
5. blue jay     robin     woodpecker

## Week 26 Activity 5     Combining Sentences

1. Jim likes chocolate chip cookies best.
2. My dog likes to run and play.
3. Cam is my best friend.
4. I have a new green dress.
5. The baby smiled and laughed at me.

## Bonus Activity: Six Silly Questions

1. Do puppies have wings?     No
2. Is the sun hot?     Yes
3. Can you read a book?     Yes
4. Do you smell with your ears?     No
5. Do you have three eyes?     No
6. Can you eat a peach?     Yes

## Week 27 Activity 1

1. I read the story of The Three Little Pigs.
2. It was funny but scary too.
3. I'm     I and am
4. he's     he and is
5. fast     slow

## Week 27 Activity 2

1. one box    two boxes
2. one dress    two dresses
3. Jaxon lost his money on the way home.
4. This year, I'm going to go to summer camp.
5. Have you ever gone to Hillwood Camp before?

## Week 27 Activity 3

1. Evan hit the ball over the fence.
2. Eddie ran fast to find it.
3. It's fun to run and play at school.
4. We play tag and ball every day.
5. swim    quack    fly

## Week 27 Activity 4

1. glow: blow, flow, slow
2. Those strawberries are red.
3. Toni and I are going to look for bugs.
4. Many (bees) fly around our (flowers).
5. (Mother robin) laid (eggs) in her (nest).

## Week 27 Activity 5 Real or Make-believe?

1. Crazy Cat flew in a red airplane.    Make-believe
2. Rover ate the food in his dish.    Real
3. A shark likes to swim.    Real
4. The parrot sat reading his book.    Make-believe
5. Boys and girls go to school.    Real

## Bonus Activity: Going Fishing

| s | a | l | m | o | n |   |   |
|---|---|---|---|---|---|---|---|
| m | u | s | k | i | e |   | h |
|   |   | n |   |   |   |   | c |
|   |   |   | f |   | b |   | r |
|   |   |   |   | i | a |   | e |
| c | a | t | f | i | s | h | p |
|   |   |   |   |   | s | h |   |
| e | k | i | p |   |   |   |   |

## Week 28 Activity 1

1. Dale's toy tractor
2. the boy's skates
3. I like chocolate, vanilla, and strawberry ice cream.
4. We took water, cookies, and sandwiches on the hike.
5. paper    paints    water

## Week 28 Activity 2

1. Mom squeezed the lemons, added water and sugar, and stirred.    Lemonade
2. Debbie and I aren't going over there.
3. Carl mixed red, purple, and white paint.
4. cry    fly    sky
5. fight    night    might    right

## Week 28 Activity 3

1. Did the bird build a nest?
2. Can you come over?
3. father
4. When will you go to the movie?
5. I am going tonight with my sister, Erin.

## Week 28 Activity 4

1. A baby dog is called a puppy/pup.
2. Jim found this dime in the yard.
3. He knew it was Franny's dime.
4. The (geese) flew in a big V.
5. Harry's pet (mice) live in a cage.

## Week 28 Activity 5

1. Put your toys (in the toy-box).
2. The books go (on the bookshelf).
3. Hang your coat (on the hook.)
4. Put your slippers (near your bed).
5. Put your crayons (in the box).

**BONUS ACTIVITY: SCRAMBLED SENTENCES**

1. On Saturday I went to a party.
2. It was Gabby's birthday.
3. We had hot dogs and cake.
4. It was fun!

**WEEK 29 ACTIVITY 1**

1. There was nothing in that old box.
2. Rover ran and hid under the bed.
3. little
4. could
5. claw, raw, paw, flaw

**WEEK 29 ACTIVITY 2**

1. Did she remember to take her two books to school?
2. I want to read the poem <u>Alligator Pie</u>.
3. We all clapped for the singer.
4. Dad is running in the big race.
5. Mary's

**WEEK 29 ACTIVITY 3**

1. My big brother hit the ball hard.
2. Isn't he a good ball player?
3. cattle     geese
4. women     children
5. The milk spilled on the floor.     Real

**WEEK 29 ACTIVITY 4**

1. Gina (doesn't) like chocolate milk.
2. We (don't) want to be late.
3. My puppy, King, grew and grew.
4. He is too big to sleep on my bed.
5. New Brunswick  3

**WEEK 29 ACTIVITY 5     SLED DOGS**

1. Sled dogs work     b) in Canada's North
2. Dogs pull the sleds     c) over the snow
3. Dogsleds are better than     b) trucks or cars
4. The driver yells     a) Mush
5. The dogs like to     c) race

**BONUS ACTIVITY: WORK AND PLAY AT SCHOOL!**

| books   Y | read   B  | play     B  | write    B  |
|-----------|-----------|-------------|-------------|
| crayons Y | pencils Y | paper    Y  | run      B  |
| desks   Y | draw   B  | scissors Y  | markers  Y  |

**WEEK 30 ACTIVITY 1**

1. A bear sleeps most of the winter.     Real
2. Helen was afraid of Brent's dog.
3. Sometimes it barks a lot at children.
4. drawing
5. orange

**WEEK 30 ACTIVITY 2**

1. start     stop     Opposite
2. Cinderella wore a beautiful dress to the palace.
3. She lost a glass slipper when she ran away.
4. outside 2
5. understand 3

**WEEK 30 ACTIVITY 3**

1. I just learned how to draw a dragon.
2. Now I am going to draw a castle.
3. Bree
4. black
5. thank

### WEEK 30 ACTIVITY 4

1. We liked the song It's a Small World.
2. Did you heard our class singing it?
3. Where do you live?
4. On my bike.              Not a Sentence
5. Your new puppy is cute.     Sentence

### WEEK 30 ACTIVITY 5

1. Ivy and (I) went to the movie.
2. My aunt gave the picture to (me)
3. The baby (made) a mess.
4. The boys (climbed) up the hill.
5. I (broke) my best toy.

### BONUS ACTIVITY: READ AND DRAW

Check for accuracy of picture/sentence match.

### WEEK 31 ACTIVITY 1

1. bug     rug     hug
2. bet     get     met
3. Will you call Mr. Drake for me?
4. I need to ask him about my homework.
5. Tuesday, May 2, 2017.

### WEEK 31 ACTIVITY 2

1. into    in    and    to
2. upstairs   up and stairs
3. Karen's bike is red and blue.
4. I'm not going to go to the game.
5. Janet put on her raincoat and boots. Was it …… rainy?

### WEEK 31 ACTIVITY 3

1. Kim and I walked (to) the playground.
2. Her little brother wanted to come (too).
3. grandmother 3
4. Robert Munsch writes funny books.
5. What is your favourite book to read?

### WEEK 31 ACTIVITY 4

1. Dad turned on the television. Then ……… he sat down to watch it.
2. I didn't see any apples in that tree.
3. Are you trying to play a trick on me?
4. Does Chloe have a new pet?   Question
5. The best score?      Not a question

### WEEK 31 ACTIVITY 5       RHYMING RIDDLES

1. I am a pet.       I rhyme with 'log'   dog
2. I am a colour.    I rhyme with 'fellow' yellow
3. I am a toy.       I rhyme with 'hall'   ball
4. I am a treat.     I rhyme with 'dandy'.   candy
5. I am a number.    I rhyme with 'door'.    four

### BONUS ACTIVITY: FIND THE MESSAGE

| I | X | l | i | k | e | Y | t | o | Z |
| p | l | a | y | X | w | i | t | h | Y |
| m | y | Z | f | r | i | e | n | d | s. |

I like to play with my friends.

### WEEK 32 ACTIVITY 1

1. Lee and I want to play at Luke's house.
2. He asked us to come over on Friday.
3. brown     town     frown
4. inside, outside     Opposite
5. big, huge     Same

### WEEK 32 ACTIVITY 2

1. The plants begin to grow.      Spring
2. Where do you and your family live?
3. I live in the green house on Elm Street.
4. The dragon breathed fire at us.   Make-believe
5. Apples grow on trees.     Real

## Week 32 Activity 3

1. Under the bed.           Not a sentence
2. Come home early.         Sentence
3. Brush your teeth and comb your hair.
4. Which shoes should I wear to Bonnie's party?
5. Sunday, August 25, 1974.

## Week 32 Activity 4

1. churches
2. Ms Green wants all the boys to help her.
3. How long will all these jobs take?
4. (She) can't reach the doll.
5. Will you please help (her)?

## Week 32 Activity 5   Picture Clues

1. You can eat an apple.
2. You can tie your shoe.
3. You can read a book.
4. You can fly a kite.
5. You can sleep in a bed.

## Bonus Activity: A Not – So – Secret Message!

| C | a | n | a | d | a |   | i | s |   | t | h | e |   | b | e | s | t |   | ! |
|---|---|---|---|---|---|---|---|---|---|---|---|---|---|---|---|---|---|---|---|
| d | b | o | b | e | b |   | j | t |   | u | i | f |   | c | f | u | t |   | ! |